DIARY OF A SEASON

DIARY OF A SEASON

Lawrence Dallaglio

Virgin

First published in 1997 by Virgin Books,
an imprint of Virgin Publishing Ltd
332 Ladbroke Grove, London W10 3AH

A catalogue record for this book is available from the British Library.

ISBN 1 85227 674 6

Typeset by TW Typesetting, Plymouth, Devon

Printed and bound by
Mackays of Chatham, Lordswood, Chatham, Kent

Contents

Foreword

So much began to happen for Lawrence Dallaglio from the time that Rob Andrew, Dean Ryan, and Steve Bates decided to leave Wasps and accept the challenge of the new-age professionalism at Newcastle. Everything was thrown into disarray at Wasps and the one person that everybody looked to, without doubt, was Lawrence. He was an individual of some character even then, and the way he went on to grip things was really remarkable for one so relatively in-experienced.

He has a great personal belief in his own ability to do a job and he is able to communicate that intensity of purpose to all those around him. Working with him, amongst the forwards at Wasps, was great because he didn't stand any messing about by the lads, and so when there was work to be done we got on and did it. He was very good at making sure the lads responded, and always led by personal example.

Nothing is ever down to one man in a rugby team, no matter how inspirational you are, but he is one of the main focal points within the successful Wasps set-up. As coaches, Rob Smith, Nigel Melville and myself have been able to tag things on around him. You meet various people throughout your life, and some of those people have an aura about them; Lawrence is one of them. When he walks into a room you are immediately aware of him and you sit up and take notice. Other people can walk through a door and nothing changes but with him you are aware of a presence; he is good-looking, he has a big physique, and he demands attention. Willie John McBride, the 1974 British Lions captain, was also like that, as was Fergus Slattery, a fellow back-row forward in that same squad. When Lawrence looks around a room the quality of his eye contact is quite piercing, it fixes people.

He has fantastic parents and towards the climax of the 1996–97 season, when Lawrence had his baby, he amused us all with stories of his mum ringing up and asking if he was OK to play – before asking about the baby!

It seemed that a great weight was lifted from his shoulders when it was finally sorted out as to what position he would play. It made a huge difference to him, and his career, when he slotted in comfortably at No. 6. It is the consistency with which he has played which I find amazing. You get some good players who are a bit in and out, who can't even play for 80 minutes at the same level. But Lawrence maintains his own levels, match by match. There is an intensity about his game, that same intensity that New Zealand bring to their game, where people are always on the boil, always there or thereabouts. If you had to state categorically what English rugby needs, it is more players like him.

At Wasps, there is a mutual agreement and understanding amongst players that this is the way we want to play, and these guys aren't just playing in ten-minute spells and then having a rest for ten; they are playing for 60, 70 and, in some cases, 80 minutes, and the one person who has been driving them forward is Lawrence. Everything spins off from his example and, in this way, he has brought the best out of his players.

He was magnificent for the Lions against South Africa in 1997, because of that same consistency he brought to his game. He was there all the time. He was one of the few Lions who was guaranteed a Test place when the squad left for South Africa, and he lived up to all of those expectations.

The future will be a challenge for him because, at the age of just 25, he has set very high standards already. I just hope, with the poundings he is giving his body, that he can carry on and steer clear of injuries. There are people in rugby who manage to do that and, hopefully, he will be one of them. I think there is a lot more to come because of his innate belief in his own ability and the fact that he can communicate that to other people and inspire confidence in them. He is a good leader on and off the field and he has high personal standards which he is capable of passing on which, in this day and age, is a vital commodity.

On a personal level, my younger son, Ben, was in Australia this year when England were there for the one-off Test match in Sydney. He rang Lawrence in the team hotel and told him he was around. Lawrence later detached himself from having breakfast with the lads and came across for a long chat; it was a nice touch.

Roger Uttley
Harrow School
July 1997

Roger Uttley played for Gosforth and Wasps and won 23 caps for England between 1973 and 1980. He played in all four Tests for the 1974 British Lions in South Africa. He went on to become England coach for the 1991 Rugby World Cup and was assistant coach on the 1989 Lions tour to Australia.

Introduction

In August 1996, every rugby player in England knew that life was never going to be the same again. The players at the top end of the game could look forward to the hardest season in the history of rugby as the first professional winter approached. Physically and mentally they were to be tested as never before, not only in the increasingly demanding domestic leagues but in Europe as well, because English clubs were taking part in European competition for the first time. At the end of the season was the enormous challenge of winning a place on the 1997 British Lions tour to South Africa, the first to that country since 1980 and the first fully professional Lions' tour.

Pre-season training at Wasps was already in full swing. Like other clubs, we had bought players and others had moved on. Like other clubs, we had a restructured organisation to tackle the new game. But we had the personal and financial backing of Chris Wright, chairman of Chrysalis, whose interest in our activities meant that Wasps became the first rugby club to play regularly on a soccer ground, QPR's Loftus Road in West London.

Some of this was running through my mind during pre-season fitness work. I also realised that it had been only a year since the International Rugby Football Board had made its declaration in Paris that the game was going open, that amateurism was finally dead and that professionalism, in all its forms, was to be the order of the day. In England, the Rugby Football Union dampened down some of the early fires of professionalism by putting in place a season-long moratorium so that a few base points could be established throughout the game. But if the RFU believed this would stop the game opening up as never before they were wrong.

There were to be massive financial changes throughout the 1995–96 season and Wasps were the first club to be affected. It was not through anything we had done ourselves, but through the decision of Sir John Hall to broaden his sporting interests in Newcastle by turning the rugby club into a fully funded professional set-up with the target of first division status and a place in Europe as quickly as possible. It caught the game, and Wasps in particular, off balance. And it was to change my life.

When I became captain of Wasps in October 1995 Rob Andrew had just moved to Newcastle for £150,000 per year on a five-year deal, and that had really set the tone for professional rugby. He was the first major player to make a big transfer deal and I think there was a worried feeling, not just at Wasps but around every club: just what sort of precedent would it set? But professionalism was here and people were going to exploit it. It was obviously a bit of a blow to Wasps and then, on top of that, Rob took away two other key players at the club, Dean Ryan and Steve Bates. I never blamed Rob for that because he had made a huge move north – geographically, domestically and financially – and anyone who leaves to join another company likes to take a few in-house workers with them. He was going up to a new environment where his character was going to be tested to the full. He needed to be surrounded by people he knew and it therefore didn't seem unnatural for him to ask Dean and Steve to go with him. In fact, Dean had told me about this three or four weeks prior to it becoming public knowledge and said to me 'What do you think about it? You know I've had this opportunity, Rob has asked me to go and coach with him – what do you think of it?' He started talking about figures and I was absolutely blown away with the sort of numbers we were talking about. Here was a guy who had left the army, played rugby and worked for DHL, and had then got himself a job with a bank earning between £20,000 and £30,000. Suddenly, there was a chance for him to do what he loved, coaching and playing rugby, and earn £75,000 a year for doing just that. It was a huge opportunity that he had to take. I told him that providing the move was right for him and his family, it was a fantastic opportunity financially. It was difficult because the whole playing structure we had set up at the club really revolved around those three players and Rob Smith, our coach.

Wasps had learnt a lesson from the England tour to South Africa in 1994. I was very much on a learning curve then and had taken a back-seat role in proceedings. The tour got off to a losing start and therefore the management was under pressure to get results. For players like myself, who only played three games out of a possible eight, it was a learning exercise. I watched the South Africans closely, from their provincial teams right down to their under-14 sides. Through witnessing their incredible skills, particularly the way they seem to move the ball so comfortably, the message hit home that we were light years behind them. We were playing all the wrong rugby and really not even trying to play the game the way it should be played. So new ideas came back to Wasps and we had possibly one of our most successful seasons ever, spearheaded by Rob Andrew, Dean Ryan, Steve Bates and Rob Smith. Even though we didn't actually win anything, we set all sorts of try-scoring records in 1994–95. We also got to the Pilkington Cup Final, and although we let ourselves down there, it was still a fair bit of progress. We beat Leicester in the semi-final, did well in the league and were full of confidence for the 1995–96 season when Rob, Dean and Steve left. The danger was that they would take away not only two or three key players, but the playing structure of the club as well. So much revolved around those players. The big Irishman Nick Popplewell followed fairly shortly afterwards and then, perhaps the most important of all, Graham Childs, although Graham's move was much more expected. He had already moved to West Hartlepool for work reasons because Nike wanted him in Sunderland – and we understood that. But Rob Andrew was quick to pick him up from West Hartlepool. It was a big blow to us – we had lost five players in all. Fortunately, because of the ethos of the club, the way Wasps have always developed their own players, we were able to bring in players like Andy Gomarsall and Nick Greenstock who had had a few chances in the team but had never been regulars.

People realised that the pressure was really on us in that first fixture against Leicester. It was a mammoth game, although there was no guarantee that we would have won the fixture with Rob Andrew and Dean Ryan in the team. I played No. 8 in the game; it just suited me better to be playing there at the time. I hadn't played No. 8 for quite some time, and it was probably no coincidence that Jack Rowell, the England coach, came to watch the game. Although we were beaten we put in a performance that showed we hadn't really lost too much of the old Wasps traits, such as the character the side had shown in the previous season. I think we were still in a state of shock. Everyone involved in rugby – certainly everyone in the First Division was thinking, 'What is going on?'

At this stage, rather than setting any targets, we were very much playing with just heart and determination and purely trying to hang on in there. We seemed to be losing players quicker than I don't know what, the question was where was it all going to stop? Was Rob Andrew going to offer me a contract? Was he going to try to take wing Damian Hopley, a key player in the future development of the club and someone who was on the verge of appearing for England? The club really had to act quickly and make people aware that something would be done in order to keep the players.

The Wasps training plans had to be restructured as well. That was done with Rob Smith carrying on as coach while

Nigel Melville was brought in as director of rugby. But the reality of what had happened really hit home the following week when we travelled up to Orrell where we've always won and won well. We lost, and having been historically up there amongst the elite of English rugby, we faced the danger of slipping down and losing our status, or at least losing the sort of aura that had taken such a long time and such a lot of hard work to create at Wasps. It was a huge worry, not only for me, but for everyone at the club. There were rumours right across the first division of big-money backers waiting in the wings and, because we were thinking that no one would want to back a club that was not successful, there was a bit of a cloud of anxiety off the field, which obviously didn't help. So the message to the players from then on in was that we would step up the training, and we agreed that all we could control was the way we played on the pitch. We were not in control off the pitch but we were in control of playing so we would get that right and concentrate on winning. It was all about survival and potential qualification for Europe. At that stage, no one even knew whether it was going to be the top four or five clubs who would qualify – that, again, was just speculation. But what we did know was that if we finished as high up in the league as possible then we would give ourselves a chance of whatever was going to be available. We were thinking purely on a game-by-game basis.

It is always invidious to single out individuals for special praise, especially in a club like Wasps, but certainly the more experienced, those I would call the senior pros or the older guard, rose to the challenge, probably in a different way to the younger players. The younger players bring the exuberance of youth, enthusiasm and ambition, but older players bring all the knowledge of years of top-class club rugby. The likes of Matt Greenwood, Richard Kinsey, Kevin Dunn and Buster White really helped to dig us out of a potentially difficult situation. They had always had one of their peers as a captain, a guy who is of a similar age and physicality. All of a sudden they've got a guy who's only twenty-three – a good few years younger than them – appointed skipper, but their reaction was absolutely superb. We forgot about personalities and just focused on making sure that we achieved the best possible results that season. The younger players were probably not aware of the sort of crisis the club might be facing. Perhaps they had not been involved in the first team and club rugby enough to appreciate what was happening. I think that sort of naïvety probably helped them a great deal because they just went out and played. But we had lost two games on the trot, Leicester and Orrell, and we had done nothing to suggest that we were about to extract ourselves from a potentially very difficult situation.

I'd been included in the England squad in November 1995, which was fantastic. It was the first time since the Second Test on the 1994 South Africa tour, where I had ended up on the bench because of the injury crisis, and it had all been a little bit unreal. But this time I was in on merit and among the squad to face South Africa at Twickenham. Even before the game kicked off I was adamant that I knew I was going to play. What had stuck in my mind was the last test we had played against them in Cape Town, where they had given us a bit of a stuffing physically – they'd really laid into us. I had also watched them throughout the 1995 World Cup – obviously, they were hugely physical and impressive. I was covering the back five positions in the pack so if any one of those was injured I was going to make my debut. I knew that they were going to come over and present a very physical challenge, and where South Africa are involved there are always plenty of bodies used and often a lot of injuries. They are a highly physical team and probably the best defenders in the world. They were going to present England with a huge challenge and I really felt involved, not just with the team but with the whole squad as well, and I thoroughly looked forward to the occasion. It made me feel that all the disappointment I had suffered over the summer after being omitted from the World Cup squad had suddenly been lifted. I had been disappointed at not going to South Africa for the World Cup but, in hindsight, saw the wisdom of the decision – you simply can't risk an uncapped player in a World Cup, especially in the crucial area of the back row. It was the dawn of a new era in English rugby and, by getting myself on the bench I was involved in the first chapter. Although some people might argue that if it was really a new era in English rugby then why was Bath's Andy Robinson recalled at open side for his eighth cap. But I feel that he had justified his place in the team and I was delighted he had the chance to represent his country again. Andy has been around for a long time; he has campaigned tirelessly for Bath, and he is an excellent role model for anyone who wants to play open side. I didn't feel disappointed at being pipped at the post by someone like him.

Going into the South Africa game, Northampton's Tim Rodber got an injury quite early on so I knew I was going to come on at some stage and, when he came off, I was very fortunate to come on at a natural restart. Their wing, Chester Williams, had just scored and it was kickoff to England: the ball went up high in the air, allowing me to go forward and make a physical statement right from the start, which is not always easy. It was a wonderful, wonderful feeling for me, but all the other England people on the field probably couldn't wait for the final whistle. From my point of view the final whistle could have been an hour away – I was absolutely elated. I had achieved a lifelong ambition, but to do that at Twickenham as well, the home of English rugby, and against the world champions ... that was a double, a triple bonus. I think my excitement was reflected in the way I played because I just wanted to get my hands on the ball as many times as possible – I had fresh legs and was full of enthusiasm and ambition. We took a series of tap penalties, and I was able to get my hands on the ball, and we managed to build up a head of steam which culminated in Phil de Glanville's try. Many people said after the game,

'Didn't Lawrence Dallaglio play well? He made an impression,' but I only had fourteen minutes of the game and, whilst I did plenty right, I didn't have time to do much wrong. From my own point of view I know that rugby is an eighty-minute game and that you can play well for 14 minutes but it's what you do for the other sixty-six that actually matters. Nonetheless, I was thrilled to bits and was hoping that perhaps the performance would project me another step up the ladder, and that next time perhaps I would be able to start the game – but that was a matter for other people to decide.

Then I had to come back down to earth and go back to Wasps, but, in a sense, because I had now made it into the England team the timing was almost perfect for my appointment as club captain. Wasps had a new England international now, and therefore a focus and a target. A lot of the younger players could now see that it is possible to get caps at as early an age as twenty-three. I think that helped everyone immensely and while I could have easily come back and wallowed in the ecstasy of playing international rugby, I knew I was coming back to a very difficult situation at the club. There was no time for swanning about and no time for prima donnas; we had to get back to the serious business of grafting, of getting some league points and ensuring that we stayed in the First Division and not only stayed there, but stayed in the top half.

The Bristol game was a turning point in the season. It was a wet, horrible, miserable afternoon – it usually is when we play at the Memorial Ground – but we managed to grind out a close result. It was my first game for the club at open side that season. I had been playing blind side up until Dean Ryan left, then I played No. 8 for the Leicester and Orrell games and then I moved to open side. It was probably the quickest route into the England team. I had a conversation with Jack Rowell during a training session where he said to me 'are you really the fastest forward in English rugby?' I think he had been given some results of some sprint tests and so I said 'I would like to think so, but we'll have to wait and see'. We had a discussion and he was obviously keen for me to start playing open side. He said, 'If you have got this pace, we've got to start using it. I feel you should be playing open side. We are going to start taping your games now and send the cassettes to Andy Robinson. He'll analyse them and they'll enable him to help you.' So there was definitely a change in thinking about the open side position – having picked Andy Robinson for his eighth cap, it seemed they were now looking more towards size, towards having a bigger back row. So the Bristol game was significant on two levels, it was a big game for the club and it was the first time I played open side at this level.

It made me laugh because at the time I knew that, out of the three back row positions, open side was not the one I wanted. I asked myself 'Are you making the right move? You've never played open side at a high level but you could possibly be picked there for the next England international. You've talked your way into being picked for the next England international.' I hadn't played my way into it, because I hadn't played at No. 7 before.

It was a very difficult situation at Wasps because I had never played at No. 7 for the club and now I was asking Rob Smith if I could play there. Also I was asking at a time when we couldn't really start messing about with the mechanics of the team because we needed to win games. He was tremendously brave by saying, 'Yes, let's have a go'. He said to me, 'Look, I don't care where you play as long as we win games.' I was pleased that they weren't trying to hold back my own development for the benefit of the team.

Next, I was driving down to England training with fellow Wasp Damian Hopley and Jason Leonard of Harlequins. We turned on Radio 5 Live and got the usual England selection procedure, they went through the team and then announced my selection against Western Samoa. The celebratory noise in the car was obviously something Jason was hearing for the fifty-sixth time. He was fairly used to seeing the highs and lows of those around him, whether they be celebrating or trying to throw themselves out of the car. I think the two of them would admit that the biggest surprise here was my selection to start a match for the first time. We were all ecstatic about that and the noise in the car was deafening. As that died down we heard Ian Robertson commenting on the team selection and then it dawned on me that I had been picked at open side.

I thought to myself that had I been picked on the left wing for England I'd have been happy to play. So I was absolutely ecstatic but knew that I would have to learn pretty quickly what I should be doing there or I wouldn't be staying too long. Having said that, as I started to train and play open side a bit more it dawned on me that what I needed to do was to make sure that I didn't do anything wrong, because at international level it is quite an unforgiving arena. One bad mistake can not only cost you your place in the team but in some situations it can cost you your international career – people start labelling you as a guy who can't tackle, as a guy who hasn't got good hands, who can't get in, can't do the dog work, etc. Once categorised, it's difficult to get out and dispel the myth that's been created. So I found myself being over-cautious and I didn't feel comfortable at all, because that's not the way I play. As a back-row forward you can't be over-cautious and as an open side you certainly shouldn't be, although you shouldn't be too hot headed either – it's just knowing when to apply caution and when to go full out.

So I certainly didn't feel totally at ease, that's for sure. Mind you, I don't think anyone would have felt totally at ease having played only one game of club rugby at open side before being thrust into the international arena and told: 'There you are son, that's your No. 7 shirt – and by the way Peter Winterbottom wore that for fifty-eight caps. Get out there and do that, but hold on we don't just want you to do what he did – we want you to do a little bit more of everything else.' So it was quite a daunting prospect to inherit that shirt. I was ready for the publicity and the public attention because I had been through that with the World Cup Sevens in 1993. And you couldn't have got more public than the Wasps' situation, which we shared with the rest of the country. I certainly felt very sharp and I was looking forward to making my first start for England and at least having the chance to make an impression on the field as opposed to sitting on the bench. My worry was that I didn't just want to play for England once – I wanted to play time and time again. I still do and I want to go on and achieve things with England and for England both individually and collectively. I'd done all the hard work to get there and now I was being given my chance. Perhaps I was fortunate that the opposition, without being disrespectful to Western Samoa, were perhaps a little bit more forgiving than some could be.

I scored a try on my debut although all I had to do was fall over the line. But to score a try on a full debut at Twickenham would help to secure my place in the team. I had a reasonable game, although probably a game that reflected the England performance. We were comfortable winners but didn't play with the shape and composure that we had come to expect. It was hard to be composed when I was playing the last game before England's Five Nations' challenge and knew that I had a real prospect of getting picked for the championship, which was tremendously exciting. I was selected for the opener against France in Paris. We were pulled into squad training at Twickenham which meant that the England management stopped me from playing the league game against Harlequins. I was training on Saturday morning whilst my team were playing Harlequins at Sudbury.

For me to miss a game is a huge blow, but to miss the London derby against Harlequins was really disappointing. Although Jason Leonard and Will Carling were missing from their team, that was no consolation. For me to be away from the team that I was captaining was hard. I knew that although we had had a good win against Bristol, things were far from right and there was still a hell of a long way to go in the rehabilitation process. We trained very hard with England and I remember coming back to the changing room to find Jason and Will looking very smug about the result. Quins ended up 34–3 winners. I just wanted to be back at the club. I didn't really want to be there. I was totally helpless in that I hadn't been able to affect the result, I hadn't been able to play, I hadn't even been able to watch. By winning at Bristol we had repaired the damage, or at least temporarily patched up the cracks that had appeared against Leicester and Orrell. But we seemed to have opened up an even bigger one with the Harlequins game. And that made life very, very difficult. I knew it wasn't due to a lack of ability because I knew the players who were there. I had seen them play well down at Bristol and play well all season. It was almost a sense that a lot of the guys had given up really, because you don't lose by scores like that – it was like Chelsea losing 7–0 to Arsenal; it just doesn't happen. As such, it was deeply disappointing.

Even though I hadn't been involved, it was a bad note on which to end the year after what had been, for me personally, a fantastic time. I'd become captain of Wasps, made my debut for England, scored my first try for England and been picked for my first Five Nations' game. I think the Wasps thing helped me keep a sense of perspective on everything. From the England point of view, although I'd broken through into the team I knew that it was very much a question of performing consistently to justify being there because the likes of Neil Back of Leicester and other open sides around the country were saying, 'Hold on a minute, what the hell are you picking this bloke for? He's only played one game at club level.' I know that if I had played six years in one position and someone who had just come along got the nod ahead of me, I would be very disappointed. Although I was very excited and very happy, there was no complacency – I think that's something I've always tried to maintain. I've never sat in a comfort zone feeling that I've achieved everything because you are always learning as a rugby player. You always have to be conscious of what's happening around you. You have just got to be aware of your surroundings really, but if you become too aware of them then you end up losing form and everything else. You have to keep moving forward as a player and not be content with one or two performances.

I began 1996 with a huge number of objectives. Wasps had not sorted out any contracts by then but they had put players on a match- and a win-bonus schedule. What we wanted to do at the club was put everyone on an even playing field and from Nos. 1–15 we were going to be paid the same. I think we were paid something like £100 a game and if we won, instead of getting £100 we got £200. It was a start, a signal, I would say; the amount was irrelevant because it was all the club could afford at the time. I think we had made a £40,000 profit from the previous season and taking into account the number of games left in the season I think the club was very honest to tell us what they could realistically do and then do it. It was a commitment the club made to its staff and I think it sent a pretty firm message to the players: 'Listen, if you play for us, the club will reward you and give you what it can afford.' But I wouldn't say the money made people approach the games any differently. Compared to the sort of figures that are bandied around today it was a very humble beginning, but it was still a sign that the club was prepared to become professional; it was prepared to forego the practice of the last 125 years and start to pay the players from day one of the new professional era.

From my discussions with various players it was clear that Wasps weren't alone in doing that. Obviously some clubs could afford to give more, and some clubs were perhaps highlighting individual players and giving them more. Players were now starting to receive phone calls from other clubs, albeit only for the very initial stages of negotiation, and therefore if a player was being given nothing then he would be far more open or receptive to offers.

At Wasps, a number of the players became natural targets for other clubs because you strike a club while it's weak, and we had certainly been hit a few times. With everything that had happened it was a chance for people to come in and try to pick off the best bits before the whole thing either sunk or stabilised. I had offers from a few clubs and I think what people admired, not just in me, but in a number of the other players at the club as well, was the loyalty that we gave to the club. I wasn't alone in receiving telephone calls; I'm sure people like Damian Hopley were well sought-after. Many of the younger players were certainly being approached by other clubs, clubs that were in a strong position and wanted to become even stronger. But our players would only leave for a club which had consistently performed at a higher level than Wasps. Anything else would be a step backwards.

Some of the offers that I received were totally ridiculous; I wouldn't even have thought of reading the contract. There was so much that was up in the air at the time, the whole game needed to stand still and have a look at itself for a second and ask 'Where are we going?' You couldn't make decisions in that atmosphere and if you had rushed into anything it could easily have backfired. I think anyone who did make quick decisions, other than someone like Rob Andrew, who was given something clear cut, was being very foolish. I didn't have to move anywhere because we weren't in a position where we were about to lose anything. No one knew what was happening with the First Division and no one knew who was going to qualify for Europe.

I'd broken into the England squad and needed to consolidate that position so I wanted to be with a successful club. If I was going to progress I needed to be playing at the highest level week in, week out and I think playing for Wasps against the top teams was the highest level. But as the season progressed the importance and potential of European rugby became apparent. European rugby would give exposure to the right facilities, the right environment, the right coaching facilities and the right competitions and would therefore offer the perfect opportunity to develop as a player. So the way I saw it was really like the rest of the squad . . . take care of the playing side, and all this contract situation, all these offers and all the ramifications of professionalism will take care of themselves in due course. The talk of contracts and offers combined with the rumour mill within rugby was all very exciting – so and so was going to buy this club, so and so was going to buy that club, this club might be playing here next season, this club might be playing there, they might be signing this player from New Zealand.

What we felt was important as a club, and certainly I did as an individual, was that because the game was going to be professional next season we needed to do what we could to make sure we took advantage of that. The best thing we could do was to play to the best of our ability and make sure that the club finished as high as it possibly could, that way we would be well placed to take advantage of the professional era.

A player who is showing good rugby skills for a club who are playing well is going to be sought after. As with any other company, if you're doing the business then people are going to want you. Fortunately, as we were getting £100 or £200 a week from Wasps, we were able to put the financial talk aside because we were being looked after. The pace at which rumours were spreading was fast and furious. It was just absolutely incredible – all of a sudden the gossip columns took an interest and the media coverage on rugby exploded.

As a club we were able to give ourselves very firm objectives post-Christmas, enabling us to cast aside everything else that was happening other than the rugby. It had been decided that the top four teams were going to qualify for Europe. Although it hadn't been cast in stone, it was taken for granted that that was what was going to happen. Therefore we were able to give ourselves a very firm objective. It was interesting that all the talk up to then had been about how it could not be a proper European competition until English clubs entered. But we'd already seen the relative success of that tournament. I'd watched the Cardiff–Toulouse final live and it was clearly something to aim for. The club felt that if it was to move forward the team had to be involved in the tournament. And it was a very achievable target. We knew we couldn't win the league, so our immediate ambition was to go as far as we could in the cup, but the primary target was to finish high enough in the league so that we would qualify for the European Cup. The commercial attractions and spin-offs from the club point of view are as valuable as the playing exposure is to its players. We knew that some sort of TV deal would be struck and therefore that the club would be better off financially.

The extra step up in class on a playing level would test the players and I think the club realised that if we were to qualify for Europe, then we would immediately be a more attractive proposition to anyone who wanted to come and play for us. We always had the same philosophy as Bath, Leicester and maybe one or two other clubs in that while the game was still amateur we weren't actively going to go out and say, 'Here's a few quid, come and play for Wasps.' People came to play for the club if they wanted to but that sort of recruitment policy is a little bit naïve today. You couldn't get away with it now, but we felt that we had a strong youth system and a strong development structure, and we only wanted people who wanted to play for the club. And I'm sure Bath were very much the same. The success of the club attracts players. The objectives had been set and we could see exactly where we wanted to be.

This coincided with Nigel Melville, a former Wasps' captain, coming down to the club. He was still coaching and training at Otley, but he'd been coming to the club after being asked by England to do some work with Andy

Gomarsall, Austin Healey and one or two others. I think he warmed to Andy the most. This was not really surprising, because Andy is a Wasps' scrum half and Nigel had played there for Wasps for many years. He probably saw Andy as the player with the most similar style to his. Nigel's reputation and his whole game revolved around his pass – he had one of the best passes you've ever seen from a scrum half. I think at the time he was working on the players' passes and he probably felt that Andy's was the closest to his. He would come down to work with Andy for an hour before club training started, and being a former Wasps player he couldn't resist hanging around and looking at what was going on. Also, being a coach at Otley, he couldn't resist trying to get some ideas for his own club. He was aware of the situation that we were in. Obviously, when you get a guy of the calibre and quality of Nigel Melville there's no point in him standing around on the sidelines. It was the same with Roger Uttley the season before. He had given up his own free time to come down once or twice a week to work with the forwards. His days of coaching England to Grand Slams were over and he easily settled back in to club life. But Nigel was in a very difficult situation: working for Otley and Wasps had to be kept strictly separate, because they're in different divisions and have different standards. He's a very honest and loyal man, he didn't want to upset anything at Otley for the sake of what was in doubt at Wasps. There was no certainty that Wasps were going to have the capacity to get him involved full time and so he had to keep a foot in both camps, which became difficult for him. Now we have a three-pronged management structure: Rob Smith, an ex-Wasps player as the head coach, Roger Uttley, a former Wasps captain, a former England captain and an ex-England coach and Nigel Melville, another former Wasps and England captain.

They have all helped in the development of the club, and they know its structure and history. They were fully aware of the potential crisis that we were facing, and they wanted to help. The clubs that are the most successful are those that build from within and keep people that know the club very well. On the other hand, it's a potentially dangerous situation when someone finishes playing for the club and then immediately starts coaching his erstwhile teammates. I would find that very difficult. There has to be a gap so that both parties can adjust to their role changes. It's not easy for players to transfer their respect for a fellow player to a coach with no track record.

Roger and Nigel had been in the shadows of the Wasps environment for a number of years, and had done some work at Richmond and Otley. The Wasps players that they had played with and grown up with had all moved on to do their own coaching. Jeff Probyn was about to go and Paul Rendall had gone to Bracknell so there was now a younger element in the team. I had never worked with Roger and Nigel before, and their infectious enthusiasm was a revelation to me. Their ability to inspire the team at any given time reflected the keen determination that comes from players who have emotional ties with the club. As former players they were part of that family and they were also people who had achieved the highest honours possible in rugby, captaincy of the British Lions and England.

As captain I wanted to be kept abreast of what was going on in finance and restructuring, particularly as it was clear that other clubs were making very definite strides to equip for the professional era. The rumours that had surrounded other clubs were now becoming reality, while the rumours surrounding Wasps were changing all the time. Not a great deal was happening but the Wasps executive assured me that things were being done to remedy the situation and make sure that we were in a position of strength going into the 1996–97 season. I think it was very difficult for those guys at the heart of the Wasps negotiating team to operate from a position of strength when they were not quite sure what was happening on the playing side. To negotiate with a prospective financier became very difficult as there were no hard and fast rules. All we had to sell was the history of the club: we won the league in 1990; we finished Pilkington Cup finalists; we had an England international in Lawrence Dallaglio; we had a very young and ambitious team. This was our grand sum really. It was all a little bit uncertain, and that made life a bit awkward.

Other clubs were starting to equip themselves quite well. Leicester were never in doubt because of their support base, their stadium has always been ahead of its time. Harlequins have always had their fingers in a number of pies and their strong links with the city meant that money was sure to be found. Bath had had the success and were too irresistible and too attractive a proposition to be missed. It left us in a difficult situation but that kept the players even more focused on the playing side: we were still in control on the pitch and knew that if we did well on the playing side we would be more likely to attract some interest in developing and financing the club.

Wasps had decided to list on AIM (the Alternative Investment Market) and float as Wasps Rugby Club. A number of the guys on the executive committee had been involved in stock market flotations before. They had seen what had happened to Chelsea FC who had done reasonably well from their flotation, so it seemed like a sensible idea and a plan was put together. This was about to go to an EGM, because EGMs were happening all over the place, when all of a sudden, at the eleventh hour the club had an approach from Chris Wright. Chris is a huge QPR fan and had been a football fan all his life. He owned Chrysalis TV, who produce *Rugby Special*, and he is an incredible sports fanatic: he owned Sheffield Sharks basketball team, he owns a football team, and he wanted to get involved in rugby. He had asked Will Carling about Harlequins but I think at that stage their deal with NEC was fairly wrapped up. Will advised him to look towards Wasps, saying that out of all the other clubs in London, we were the one to go for. Chris came up with a proposal and the plans were changed.

We were due to announce the flotation and here was Chris Wright saying he wanted to buy 49.1% of the club. The members were absolutely stunned – we were all stunned – and all of a sudden we had the prospect of playing at Loftus Road. I think Chris Wright would be the first person to admit that he didn't want to buy Wasps on its own – a future of Wasps playing at Sudbury did not appeal to him. I think the appeal to him was the merger of the two clubs, the synergy between rugby and football, between Wasps and Queens Park Rangers at Loftus Road. The opportunity to attract people throughout the M40 corridor and give Wasps a firm London identity in a catchment area probably better suited to rugby than Sudbury was obvious.

Loftus Road has wonderful commercial facilities, and also the sort of ground ideal for Wasps. We had always boasted that we liked to play expansive rugby, that we wanted to play a running game. We had always been a team that played the game in a positive manner and now potentially we had the opportunity to play on a great pitch. Sudbury, for all its tradition and all its rugby atmosphere, was very badly equipped to cope with the changes in rugby. We would now have the best club rugby stadium in the country, and certainly the best pitch. The players absolutely love it now. But then it was all still an if, because it was only going to happen if Chris Wright could buy Queens Park Rangers. There was also a slight technical hitch in that the members had to agree to the move. The prospect of losing years of tradition and heritage at Sudbury was something that could cause great unease. Wasps finished a strong fourth in the league and qualified for Europe. Now we could all look forward to an exciting new season as professional players at Loftus Road. I went to Loftus Road at a very early stage and was in awe, the prospect of playing rugby there was just mind blowing.

1 A Good Start

Our final preparations for the coming season were at a tournament in Leiden, Holland, where we beat St Mary's, Dublin 71–11 and Stade Français 44–26, scoring 16 tries in our first game. Soon it would be Sale away and the start of the Courage League. We felt that the pre-season tour had prepared us well and given an indication of how we were going to do in the league.

It was felt that we should try and fit in a game before going to play Sale. In the past we had simply phoned Saracens up, and organised a controlled game. The relationship between the clubs has always been quite good but this year the game was never likely to happen. We ended up playing amongst ourselves, firsts against seconds, just to get an idea of what we were doing.

My role as captain was to be a lot different from the one that I had taken the previous season. When I took over the captaincy, I was much more involved in the selection process and Rob Smith and I would discuss things after games. Although my view is still considered, the selection process is now done at a higher level and it's effectively out of my hands. I don't mind at all, because it involves dealing with people's livelihoods and that's a big responsibility. Players still come up to me and say they think they've been unfairly treated in selection, but they know I'm not a selector. I think that's crucial, and my place in the team is under scrutiny just as much as theirs. That is the way we have chosen to operate at Wasps.

31 AUGUST 1996

Courage League Division One: Sale 31 Wasps 33

The game was huge. We've never lost to Sale in the league, but we have always had very clean, open, hard games against them, and, away from home, it's always been very, very difficult. These were probably the two most important points that we won all season. If we had got off to a losing start, especially with games against Saracens, Bath and Leicester following pretty shortly afterwards, confidence would have been low. If you go three or four games and then you lose one, it's not the end of the world, but if you lose your first one it's very difficult to stop morale from slipping.

The objective has always been to break the Bath–Leicester monopoly and if you start by losing to Sale, you're not on the right track. We scored a try in injury time, through Andy Gomarsall, and converted to win the game 33–31. It was the most significant result of the day in terms of what it might say about the future of the season. I knew Sale could eventually have a major say in the championship and qualification for Europe. They were desperately disappointed to have lost to us, because they felt they should have won the game – but they took heart from the performance and went on to have a good season. Equally, the way we were able to pull out a performance like that and win against the odds indicated that we had a certain ability. We knew that we had let ourselves down, that we hadn't played well and we knew that perhaps the combination between certain pairings wasn't quite right. But we won and that was something that perhaps the Wasps of old wouldn't have done. The result was remarkable when you consider that we had gone to Sale with the intention of playing Scottish international lock forward Damian Cronin. However, Damian unfortunately turned his ankle practising line-outs on the Saturday morning.

Chris Wright had come up for this game, and probably

wondered what he had invested in. He saw us win, but he obviously had some serious doubts in his mind about the wage bill. Gomarsall played very well and early on in the season was by far the best scrum half in the country. Dewi Morris, the former England scrum half who had decided to come out of retirement, played opposite him. He played very well in that game and was an inspiration to Sale all season.

Sale 31 Wasps 33

Sale	*Wasps*
J Mallinder	J Ufton
D Rees	P Sampson
G Stocks	N Greenstock
M Birt	L Scrase
T Beim	S Roiser
J Baxendell	G Rees
D Morris	A Gomarsall
P Smith	D Molloy
S Diamond	K Dunn
A Smith	I Dunston
J Fowler	M Greenwood
D Baldwin	N Hadley
D O'Grady	M White
C Vyvyan	P Scrivener
A Morris	L Dallaglio

Scorers
Sale. Tries: O'Grady, Beim (2), Rees. Penalties: Stocks (3). Conversion: Stocks.
Wasps. Tries: Sampson, Gomarsall (2). Penalties: Rees (4). Conversions: Rees (3).

8 SEPTEMBER 1996

Courage League Division One: Wasps 36 Saracens 21

This was the first match we played at Loftus Road. It was Chris Wright v. Nigel Wray, the businessman and new owner of Saracens. It was not just an important game for Wasps – it was an important game for rugby in general. It would gauge the interest in professional rugby and indicate whether Sunday rugby was going to work – and whether the concept of putting Wasps in a football stadium was going to work. Were people prepared to pay the sums of money that were being asked to come and watch the matches? What was the atmosphere going to be like? Was rugby going to work in the stadium? What sort of performance were Wasps going to put out against the big-name signings of Saracens like Australian legend Michael Lynagh and French maestro Philippe Sella?

It was important that we remained the team to beat in London and, from a playing point of view, that's what the game was all about. The crowd was in the region of 8,000–9,000 people which was deemed a success. The atmosphere that they created really was something a bit special for Wasps, and also for first division rugby. The only time crowds like that had been seen before was at Leicester or a full house for a big game at Bath.

Cronin, Sheasby, King and Mitchell were all making their debuts and I think holding them back from the Sale game gave them real drive. They realised that we weren't going to pick players just because of their reputation, and that they would have to prove their worth week in, week out, so they were champing at the bit. Sheasby was particularly hacked off that he'd been left out of the team at Sale. He had played in the seconds which he hadn't enjoyed because he felt that he was an automatic selection.

There was a tremendous amount of excitement and anticipation. I hadn't even been in the changing room at Loftus Road before. The atmosphere was fantastic. All the other league games had been played on Saturday so all the attention was on us. *Rugby Special* covered the game so it was a big opportunity for us to make a statement about the club and announce our new identity as Wasps in West London. We felt we needed to give the surroundings the performance they deserved, and that was the key to our performance.

Saracens felt that they were capable of competing, and, I think, whereas in the past it was almost our God-given right to beat them, they now possessed a genuine threat. We have respected them in the past and enjoyed some very close encounters, but they had never offered quite such a hard challenge before. They had Kyran Bracken and Michael Lynagh at half-back – both world-class players – and they've always had a competent back row. I have a tremendous amount of respect for their back row because I have played with Richard Hill and Tony Diprose at England under 21 level, although up to now their talents have mainly been on show in the Second Division. It was time for them to start doing it in the First Division and it's going to be interesting to see how they get on. There is a tremendous amount of rivalry between us because we are all the same age.

The turning point of the game was Lynagh going off injured. I think that many seemed to think it was because of a tackle I had made on him but in fact fly half Alex King made the decisive blow. It was about fifteen to twenty minutes into the game when he broke right down the blind side; I hit him with a tackle and then he ran into Alex King on the next move. He got dumped and landed on his shoulder. It made a huge difference to them. When you haven't played many games together it is difficult, but when you haven't played together and then you lose your fly half it is very difficult. Bracken had to move to stand off and they were struggling all the time after that. We ended up comfortable winners, scoring three tries. The way we played, giving the ball a lot of width, we looked competent in a number of areas. Sheasby was man of the match, he had an absolutely outstanding game, he was everywhere on the pitch, and all the doubts that had crept in after the Sale performance had been addressed.

Wasps 36 Saracens 21

Wasps	Saracens
G Rees	A Tunningley
P Sampson	K Chesney
N Greenstock	P Sella
A James	S Ravenscroft
S Roiser	R Wallace

A King
A Gomarsall
D Molloy
S Mitchell
W Green
M White
D Cronin
M Greenwood
L Dallaglio
C Sheasby

M Lynagh
K Bracken
R Andrews
G Botterman
P Wallace
J Green
P Johns
A Copsey
R Hill
A Diprose

Scorers
Wasps. Tries: Mitchell, Gomarsall, Rees. Penalties: Rees (6). Dropped goal: King.
Saracens: Tries: Hill, penalty try. Penalty goals: Lynagh (2), Tunningley. Conversion: Tunningley.

Replacements
Saracens: M Lynagh replaced by D Edwards (29 minutes), J Green replaced by D Zaltman (68), P Wallace replaced by D Olney (76)
Wasps: C Sheasby temporarily replaced by R Kinsey (56–63 minutes)

The changes we made were positive and the people we brought in did a very good job. I think that performance was the lift-off that catapulted us into changing the way we wanted to play. We realised what our strengths were: we knew we had a prolific goal kicker because Canadian specialist Gareth Rees didn't miss much at all. We knew we had a back row that could compete with anyone. Alex King looked perfectly at home at fly half and as if he'd been there a long time. Andy Gomarsall continued to press his claim for an England place at scrum half and played even better than he had done at Sale the previous week – he looked very sharp and active. We had been worried and so were now much relieved, not just about the London power struggle but also because the whole venture had been successful.

If everything off the field could be matched with the quality of performance that was evident in parts of the Saracens game then the future of Wasps at Loftus Road was a bright one. The whole feeling – we had some really positive press after the game – was that Wasps had got off to a cracker. It was a far cry from the two points we managed to sneak at Sale the previous week, but league rugby is about taking the game each week and we were delighted – we were two from two. People were hungry and competitive and we were about to go down to Bath confident of victory. The feel-good factor was definitely up with Wasps. Chris Wright was happy with what had happened. He was delighted with the response to the marketing campaign and must have felt that he had made the right decision.

At Loftus Road, we only knew where the changing room was and how to get from there to the pitch. We didn't know where the bars were, nor the players' lounge. But the whole post-match atmosphere is now very different to how it used to be. Now there are contractual obligations and players are duty-bound to go and see sponsors. So, before you see your parents or your family or anyone else, before you get to a bar, you have to go and spend ten minutes with the sponsors. As captain I went to see match sponsor, National Cash Registers (NCR) who were also club sponsors, so there were all the jokes flying around – that we can keep a tab on where the money is going, if NCR are sponsors.

I spent ten minutes talking to them while the other players went to various boxes and, quite interestingly, some players went to the members' bar as well, to make sure they weren't neglected. The feeling at Wasps is very much that, after the game, the members and supporters should be able to mingle with the players and talk to them freely. In football the crowds are in and out. The stewarding company at Loftus Road had no idea of the way rugby crowds respond, the way that in rugby, once you are in the ground, there is freedom of movement; you don't need to flash your ticket to anyone to go anywhere at a rugby game, you can just wander around freely, do what you want, go from bar to bar. The stewards started off policing the rugby match in exactly the same way as they would police a football match and that put a lot of noses out of joint. Members were told that they could only go in one section of the ground and that they weren't allowed anywhere else. They weren't allowed to take their pints of beer anywhere, they weren't allowed to do this and that and it seemed to take twice as long to get in anywhere as it did before. In actual fact I think people were still wandering in after kickoff because of the extra security. The issue has now been addressed because people soon realised that rugby and football cultures are very different. It was just as much a culture shock for the Loftus Road stewards as it was for rugby followers to be attending a football ground. But these were only teething problems which have now largely been resolved. At training on Monday we said that we felt there had been too much hassle. But we had to be patient.

The signing of Va'aiga Tuigamala – ex-New Zealand, Wigan and now Western Samoa – indicated the respect that Nigel Melville had in the marketplace. I'd met Inga, as he is known, many times before, and watched him play. I'd played with him in a touch sevens tournament in Richmond about two years previously, just after he signed to play Rugby League for Wigan, and witnessed some of the skills that you don't often see in the heat of international rugby on the pitch. I got a feel for his professional attitude. He talked to me then about a knee injury which he had got playing sevens, and I think he was back playing again within four months. Usually people take six months to a year out of the game, but he was back so quickly. That's a testament to how he looks after himself. My next meeting with him was at the Middlesex Sevens final when he played for Wigan and I played for Wasps. It was quite amusing because they put him in the scrum. They said to him, 'You play Union so you can go in the scrum, you tell us what it's all about. You keep telling us how easy it is.' So Sean Edwards put him in, propping against me. I wouldn't consider myself new to the sevens game or to sevens' scrummaging. I don't think he particularly enjoyed it, and although Wigan came out victorious, I think we ruffled a few feathers and dented a few reputations. I would like to think that the episode contributed to his decision to join Wasps. Obviously the financial side had to be right for him but that wasn't something I ever got involved in.

I like to think he came to the club because he saw Wasps as having the right sort of environment for him to do well, and there's no doubt he enjoyed wearing black, seeing as much of his success in rugby had come while wearing an All Blacks shirt. The prospect of wearing a black shirt again was not only getting him excited but all the marketing men at Wasps as well. There were a number of reasons why he came – the financial side, the playing side and the playing philosophy of the club. He also saw a number of young players here and saw how he could contribute in a sort of paternal way, if you like, and pass on a lot of his experience. I don't think he ever envisaged coming back to Union so quickly – he probably felt that the way things were going to work out with his contractual obligations, he'd have to go back to Wigan and play another season there and then perhaps consider coming back to Union full time. So from the point of view of what he was looking to do, I think the marriage between Wasps and Inga was a very fortunate one.

We've never been able to attract the big names to Wasps for one reason or another, and much of the talent that we've had has been homegrown. Rob Andrew, for instance, made his name at Wasps after coming through the ranks. But now, not only had we attracted a big name but possibly the biggest name in rugby union. There was tremendous excitement and it was a firm indication of Chris Wright's intentions for the club: if the right player came along money would be provided to purchase him. It really gave everyone a tremendous lift because of his reputation within rugby – it focused everyone's mind. It all coincided with professionalism, but what Inga brought to the club wasn't only on the commercial side but on the playing side as well. He changed the philosophy and the attitude of many of the players, including myself. He re-educated a number of the players and, I imagine, some of the coaches, as to how a professional rugby player should behave – how he should look after himself, his attitude towards his work, his training and his playing philosophy. He showed what a modern professional rugby player should be.

Off the pitch, Inga conducted himself in a manner that had never been seen at a rugby club before, especially in terms of the religious aspect of his character and the general goodness in him. People fed off his religious strength. The unmistakable wrist band with the fish and the cross on it was a constant reminder of his beliefs. You definitely got the feeling that when Inga was playing, God was on your side. He made no secret of the fact that he prayed on a number of occasions that we would win, and he prayed on a number of occasions that he would be fit to play. And sure enough he was. Players were not used to that sort of thing and initially said it was stupid but you wouldn't say that to Inga himself. Ironically the one league game we lost while he was around was at Gloucester when he was unable to play. One can point to that and say we went five league games unbeaten and then we went down to Gloucester and Inga wasn't playing so we lost. But his absence wasn't the only reason. We had a poor referee, we had a player sent off – there were a number of reasons. Inga came at a time when we couldn't have asked for a better focus, with the team going to Bath and then Leicester in consecutive weeks and struggling for higher honours.

11 SEPTEMBER 1996

Anglo-Welsh League: Bridgend 32 Wasps 28

Everyone was talking about the concept of Anglo-Welsh rugby and whether or not it was going to be a requirement for the top players. We put out a mixed side in our game at Bridgend. Inga wanted to see some of the players play, which was an indication of his interest and commitment. He was prepared to sit in the car for three and a half hours, watch a near second-string side running out against

Bridgend in an Anglo-Welsh tournament in order to get a feel for the team spirit, to get a feel for some of the guys, to learn people's names and perhaps to delight some of the younger supporters who must have been thrilled to see him. The pair of us were sitting in the stand watching the game and Inga caused a lot of excitement, as expected. We were talking about the game and where he felt we were going right and wrong. We ended up losing the match 32–28 in the last minute when a kick was charged down and they scored a try. Bridgend put out their strongest side – they took the fixture very seriously – and their star back Gareth Thomas played and scored a couple of tries. Our guys were bitterly disappointed because for a lot of them it was an opportunity to get into contention for the first team. Many of them obviously felt that when the captain and one of the biggest signings in rugby union had come to watch the game that they should have made sure that they won. So in some ways it was a bit disappointing to make that journey down to Wales on a Wednesday night. You have to win those games because it's hard enough just going down there.

From the club's point of view, if we lift the Anglo-Welsh Cup it's not of any significance if we don't qualify for Europe and finish respectably in the league. So it was pretty clear that a number of the first team would not be playing Anglo-Welsh games. We've heard little or nothing of the competition since then. There was the fiasco with Neath cancelling later on and it seems that we were prepared to go down to Bridgend to play a game while they were not prepared to come all the way back up again.

14 SEPTEMBER 1996

Courage League Division One: Bath 36 Wasps 40

I've beaten Bath at home and lost heavily to them in the Pilkington Cup Final so I've seen both sides of the coin; I've felt what it's like to win and to lose against them. But on this occasion, I don't think we were really carrying the same emotional baggage as perhaps we had in the past. We had a really good feel in the team with new players like Mitchell, Rees, Sheasby, King and Inga – nearly 60% of the side had changed. A number of players had only been involved in one or two fixtures against Bath, and one of those was a victory, so the place was not a fortress for any of those guys. Having performed so well against Saracens we were confident that we could win. The hype leading up to the game was all about Inga against Henry Paul and Jason Robinson, Bath's wonderful former Rugby League players.

Both Paul and Robinson had played mid-week against Swansea and I think Bath made a bit of a mistake as a result – they got carried away with those two players. Bath cut Swansea to ribbons, and I congratulate them on that, but they got a bit overexcited by their game plan – they were throwing the ball everywhere. That was fine against Swansea because there wasn't a lot of tackling going on. Bath then came into the Wasps game feeling overconfident, still on the wave of euphoria because of the success and potential of their League boys. They played Robinson on the left wing and Paul at centre, which was fine by us because they dropped Phil de Glanville which we found absolutely staggering. They dropped Andy Robinson – he'd been the bane of our life, the main reason we'd lost so many games to Bath. And they dropped Martin Haag as well.

Andy Robinson had always made it very difficult for us. He'd been the difference between the two sides, largely because of his ability to slow our possession down. That is not to belittle his attacking qualities as he is a very good attacking player, but he certainly knew how to stop Wasps playing. Inga told me about Jason Robinson and what he was like as a person, and about what Henry Paul likes to do, and said 'Don't worry we'll keep those two in check.' I just couldn't believe the side they announced. We were talking about league rugby – Wasps v. Bath, a huge game. Winning that early encounter, in the third league game of the season, can go on and make or break the club's season and that proved to be the case. If we had lost, I think the Leicester game at home would have been a very difficult one. I was purring with excitement when they named their team. To leave Haag out – he's a stalwart and has been a fantastic player for Bath. To leave Robinson out. To leave de Glanville out and Adebayo as well. These were four anchor men who had been involved in nearly every success that Bath had had over Wasps in the last few years. Adebayo scored countless tries against us, Robinson stopped us scoring, Haag won an endless amount of ball, and de Glanville was the captain, so it didn't make sense to me.

Jerry Guscott captained the side. It certainly looked from the outside that things at Bath were a little bit wrong. We actually said that we would win this game, that they had made a bit of a mistake leaving these guys out. The feeling was there. We were already buzzing because we had enjoyed such a good performance against Saracens. It was a glorious day, beautiful sunshine, the ground was nice and hard – there could be no excuses. In the past we have gone there when it's been flooded in November and December but this time there was no excuse for either side not producing a highly entertaining game of rugby.

The team went together on the bus. Normally, a lot of guys would go direct, but nowadays that is increasingly becoming a thing of the past. Get the teams together with everyone in the same kit – it's a sense of group identity, a sense that you've got respect for each other. You don't panic at the last minute because you're organised. It all helps to build a team spirit. Bath are quite the opposite. They have never bothered to wear blazers, jackets or ties or give the opposition the same type of respect that other sides do, and yet they've been very successful. Perhaps it's just the individual statement that each player likes to make there. But we don't do that. We've got a proud identity as a club. We're not ashamed to wear something with the Wasps logo on it, even if the other twenty players are wearing the same thing. We arrived at our hotel nice and relaxed. I think everyone realised this was the biggest test to date. But that is why we play. The excitement you get before these games is unparalleled in domestic rugby and while everyone still wants to beat Bath, now everyone wants to beat Wasps as well. We were absolutely determined to win.

We had an exciting pair of half-backs playing to a good standard, so we worked to keep and recycle the ball, and go out and play. Aggressive defence was the key to it. We knew Bath liked to spin the ball, to get it through their hands, but we felt that if we put them and, in particular, Mike Catt under pressure, they might struggle. The idea was to use Inga only when and where necessary but mainly to pressurise them constantly, to make big tackles. We knew the line-out would match up and, if anything, that we had an edge in the scrums.

The hype leading up to the game meant that all eyes were on Inga, Henry Paul and Jerry Guscott, with people wondering if Guscott was up to the task. Guscott v. Inga. Inga's presence helped Nick Greenstock as well. The focus was definitely on the midfield. I only wish Phil de Glanville had been playing because it would have been him and Jerry against Inga and Nick Greenstock which would have been interesting. Jerry handled it very well. The first time Inga got the ball and ran it, Jerry put in a tackle, something which I hadn't seen for a while. He really knocked him over. I think Inga was looking forward to playing against Jerry as while he was playing Rugby League he probably thought he would never get the opportunity. Jerry rose to the occasion and tackled superbly at the beginning. It was a very fast pace, very frantic with big tackles going in and a lot of turnovers because guys were making such big tackles. We capitalised on this and Paul Sampson was allowed a run down the right wing, where he showed the sort of pace that took him into the England squad. Jerry didn't even bother trying to catch him. I think he realised it was futile and wouldn't have looked too good on camera so he tracked him back and made sure he didn't go right underneath the posts.

Andy Nicol has been the difference when Bath have been playing well. He was particularly sharp and made them look really good. He was taking penalties, changing the emphasis of attack, moving the focal point wider, putting in some super miss-passes. Andy was injured soon after the game, and that coincided with Bath's worst period of the season. I think he's their best player. He instigated their fight back just before half time and we ended up 16–14 down, having had the balance of play in the first half. But 16–14 is nothing. The belief was there and I told the players to keep tackling, to keep the pressure on and they will make mistakes. We would force them into making mistakes and then we would capitalise on that. And I felt that we were going to win the game.

Whatever I said at half time didn't quite have the desired impact and had perhaps been bettered by Jerry Guscott's pep talk as they came out and really upped the pace at the beginning of the second half. They seemed relentless although their desire to move the ball wide seemed to be a bit too frantic. But they established, they got a couple of penalties, they scored a try in the corner, and all of a sudden they were fourteen points up. We were really under the cosh at fourteen points down with half an hour to go. A tackle on the line just denied their wing Adebayo but it was looking pretty ominous. For some reason, Bath got too excited by their own ability to run the ball when all they needed to do was shut down. If Catt had kicked a couple of times for the corner, and really put us under pressure, I think we would have struggled to come back. But all credit to Bath and to Catt, they wanted to keep playing flowing rugby. Instead of kicking a few times when they were under pressure, they tried to run the ball and we stuck with our defensive pattern and put them under more pressure. Then they started to make mistakes – they were knocking on and they were getting turned over, and within another ten minutes we were back on level terms. Jason Robinson seemed to be running quite laterally because of his Rugby League temperament, and he was being closed out. We were kicking off to him in the right-hand corner, and he was catching it as he would in Rugby League and virtually running sideways. He was getting knocked down in midfield and losing possession and we were taking advantage. To me, it was a super comeback because with about ten minutes to go, we scored a converted try and a penalty to put us sufficiently in front. We made a couple of pretty good tackles. Inga was marshalling the defence and making sure they were up with him in midfield, and they were drifting. Bath were going nowhere really and we were knocking them down. Gomarsall passed to Shane Roiser, he fed Sheasby down the blind side and we outstripped them and scored. And then Gareth Rees banged over a penalty which was a huge kick, almost from the halfway line. Bath never gave up. But they were over-complicating it. When you throw the ball wide not only do you pass the ball, you also pass on the responsibility to keep the ball, and if people get tackled and don't keep hold of it, then it's a high risk game. If you get turned over and you haven't got support it can be very expensive.

Alex King dropped a simple goal in what was only his second league game; it was the biggest game he'd ever played and he looked totally at home. When he had the ball he distributed it intelligently. I believe the sign of a good half-back is the ability to keep your team going forward even when the front row are under pressure and, on this occasion, Alex displayed the necessary tactical awareness to achieve just that.

Even though we felt there were still too many mistakes, there was a belief there that we were going to win – something which had perhaps been lacking in the past. To have come back from a deficit like that was excellent. I think there was a new edge to our tackling and that was the difference between the two sides. Bath had come up against a side that was knocking them backwards and putting them under pressure and they weren't able to put the same continuity and ball retention skills together that they had against Swansea. We really put them under pressure and this enabled us to capitalise on their mistakes. To go there so early on in the season and get a result was an indication of our own ability.

When you go down to Bath and they win, the place is mobbed. I love the Bath players dearly; socially they are a great group of people, tremendous guys and I get on really well with them. When they win, the bar is crawling with them, and it's buzzing. I wouldn't be the only guy to say this, they're the first to buy you a drink and so on. But when they lose, you don't see too many of them. I think they go over to the stand and hang their heads in shame in the privacy of a box. It's not often they are beaten which is probably why they take it so badly. I think that when you lose a game like that you have to show the team that beats you some respect, but Bath have got too much pride to do that. We certainly didn't get carried away. We didn't stay down there too long, we all came back on the coach together and had a few drinks, but nothing out of hand. The reality was that we were training first thing Monday morning and we knew that we had Leicester the following week, which was to be an even tougher game for us. It was then that we realised that we had a real opportunity to do well this season.

Bath 36 Wasps 40

Bath	*Wasps*
J Callard	G Rees
J Sleightholme	P Sampson
J Guscott	N Greenstock
H Paul	V Tuigamala
J Robinson	S Roiser
M Catt	A King
A Nicol	A Gomarsall
D Hilton	W Green
G Dawe	S Mitchell
J Mallett	D Molloy
N Thomas	M White
B Cusack	M Greenwood
N Redman	D Cronin
S Ojomoh	L Dallaglio
E Peters	C Sheasby

Scorers
Bath. Tries: Robinson, Catt, Nicol, penalty try. Penalties: Callard (4).
Conversions: Callard (2).
Wasps. Tries: Sheasby (2), Sampson, Mitchell. Penalties: Rees (3).
Conversions: Rees (4). Dropped goal: King.

Replacements
Bath: H Paul replaced by A Adebayo (46 minutes).
Wasps: W Green replaced by M Griffiths (74).

A hard edge to the team was developing and, while we
realised we weren't going to go unbeaten in the season, we
certainly knew that we were going to be a difficult side to
beat. I think that gave everyone confidence for the Leicester
game. There was a respect for each other's talents and
abilities and it was recognised that the team's newcomers
were fitting in very nicely. Rees was hitting penalties; King
was proving to be a very accomplished player at fly half, a
coveted position at Wasps; Chris Sheasby was showing the
sort of speed and commitment to club rugby that he had
shown for Harlequins over the last two seasons; Inga
brought confidence and belief – he also brought out the best
in the players around him; Damian Cronin was winning the
ball for me and the team, which was exactly what we
wanted; Buster White was playing out of his socks at
flanker, as he has done for a number of years now. Things
were looking good. Slowly but surely, things were coming
together. There was genuine excitement at the club but we
weren't getting carried away. It felt as though we had been
together for such a long time, as if we were well into the
season.

22 SEPTEMBER 1996

Courage League Division One: Wasps 14 Leicester 7

This fixture came at the right time. Neil Back wasn't
playing, which was critical, but I think one of the most
important things was that Bob Dwyer, although fully on
board as coach, had not quite settled down into his job at

Leicester. He was still toing and froing between England and Australia and he hadn't returned when we played Leicester. I think his absence was significant and may well have contributed to their shapelessness.

Leicester have the biggest travelling support of any club in the First Division so we were expecting a reasonable crowd. We had about 12,000, which was great for the game and great for Wasps. I think Leicester genuinely liked playing at Loftus Road. I have spoken to some of their players since and they clearly enjoyed it; they're used to playing in that kind of environment every week so they shouldn't have felt too far away from home. Nice tight ground, big atmosphere, four stands, big stadium.

Back was absent, as was Dwyer and we were still very much in the embryonic stage of the season. Leicester had some new players in key positions, Austin Healey had signed at scrum half and Will Greenwood at centre. The big Irishman Eric Miller was playing No. 7; although I think No. 8 is his best position. They were still trying to find that bit of shape. We were a little bit more cohesive, perhaps a match or two further down the line. They had Dean Richards at No. 8, which we felt was a weakness as we could exploit that by using Sheasby at the back of the scrum. We knew that they weren't going to possess the pace threat from the back of the scrum that other sides did.

We were fortunate Steve Lander was refereeing. You need a good referee when you play Leicester, because they slow the ball up and stop you playing. They're very strong in the tackle so you have to get your body position 100% right. The key is getting to ground early because, if you don't, they'll hold you up, turn you over and someone will come in and pinch the ball off you – and they're very good at turnovers. Once they turn you over they'll either kick to the corner or counterattack. What we needed was a referee who was going to penalise them if they tried to put their hands on the ball when we went to ground, and Steve Lander penalised them several times. That enabled us to put territorial pressure on them, which was essential. You have to play a territorial game and keep them pinned down in their own half because once they start playing the touchlines and getting up the field and getting a rumble on, it's difficult to stop them. In the first half we spent about the first ten minutes in their 22 but didn't score. They cleared, came up field, got a scrum and scored a try in the right-hand corner and all of a sudden they were 5–0 up. Clearly we were going to have to keep the pressure on and take points. Then we came back to score a try and the game was quite evenly balanced at 7–5 in their favour for some time. Then they executed a back move which worked but, fortunately for us, someone threw a forward pass and the try was disallowed. It was about ten minutes from the end of the game and had the try stood, it would have killed us off.

I have always believed that you have to make Leicester play catch-up rugby because if you get in front against them they can struggle. They start to doubt themselves and then you can put up a defensive wall. Historically, they have always conceded the fewest tries in the league. They're the misers of the First Division. They defend very well – they give penalties away but they don't give tries away if they can help it. To play catch-up rugby against them is very difficult because they keep the scoreboard ticking over with a penalty here and a penalty there. So once we were in the lead we tried to keep it simple, but then in the last couple of minutes we scored a try in the right-hand corner. Gomarsall threw a dummy and gave the ball to Phil Hopley, Damian's brother who had come on for Sampson. Phil hadn't expected to be involved in the team and had probably been out the night before celebrating – he was getting married fairly shortly so he was certainly enjoying himself – but he came on and scored the winning try.

Our confidence from the Bath game helped us to this victory. Although Leicester were disorganised and without cohesion they were still a very hard side to break down. But from then on, they went from strength to strength. Bob

Dwyer must have been sent a copy of the video because he really pulled his finger out and told them a few home truths about what they were doing wrong. Another factor in our victory was that Cronin managed to keep the 6 ft 7 in Martin Johnson in check. If you are going to beat Leicester, you have to keep him quiet. Time and time again, he's an enormous presence for both Leicester and England. You're never going to completely stop him from winning balls, because Richard Cockerill throws the ball very well, but you need to pinch the odd one or two and when he does catch it you have to make sure they don't get a rumble on.

Bath and Leicester have never been beaten in consecutive weeks by anyone so we were pushing the standards up. I think that if the Bath result gave us confidence, then the Leicester result perhaps made us a little bit over-confident. It was a unique position for a lot of us. But we weren't sitting at the top of the league on our own because Harlequins had had some easy fixtures and so they were up there with us. The layout of the league table had a totally new look to it. Harlequins were top, we were second. To see such a geographical shift in power, although we realised it was early days, helped us get carried away with our own achievements and, in the end, that contributed to our downfall in Europe.

Wasps 14 Leicester 7

Wasps	Leicester
G Rees	J Liley
P Sampson	S Hackney
N Greenstock	W Greenwood
V Tuigamala	S Potter
S Roiser	R Underwood
A King	R Liley
A Gomarsall	A Healey
D Molloy	G Rowntree
S Mitchell	R Cockerill
M Griffiths	D Garforth
M White	J Wells

D Cronin	M Johnson
M Greenwood	M Poole
L Dallaglio	E Miller
C Sheasby	D Richards

Scorers
Wasps. Try: Hopley. Penalties: Rees (3).
Leicester. Try: penalty try. Conversion: J Liley

Replacements
Wasps: P Sampson replaced by P Hopley (40 minutes), C Sheasby temporarily replaced by P Scrivener (13–15 minutes).
Leicester: S Hackney replaced by M Jones (64), D Richards replaced by W Drake-Lee (81).

28 SEPTEMBER 1996

Courage League Division One: Orrell 27 Wasps 44

When you play sides like Orrell people are always expecting a slaughter. They all say it's a chance to get the points difference up. I think that's a dangerous way to approach games. League rugby is fundamentally about winning and we went up there to win the game. I was disappointed with our defence; we let them in. We were cruising at one stage at 41–0 but we let them come back and score some late tries. All our games until then had been quite close so it was important that we started to put some breathing space between points scored and points against. It was disappointing because it was due to little lapses in concentration that they scored so many. Leaving tackles to other people let them in for a couple of scores. Perhaps all the hard work that had gone into beating Bath and Leicester wasn't being maintained against Orrell.

We had still scored six tries and were pleased that we had won 44–27 but we were now looking at our own performance in a lot more detail. We began to break down our own game, and analyse each missed tackle. There are things in the game that we can't control: the referee, the environment, the weather, things like that, but we can control our own performance – and we felt we hadn't done so on the day. We had let it slip.

Orrell 27 Wasps 44

Orrell	*Wasps*
R Hitchmough	G Rees
J Naylor	L Scrase
L Tuigamala	N Greenstock
D Lyon	V Tuigamala
N Heslop	S Roiser
M Strett	A King
S Cook	A Gomarsall
M Worsley	D Molloy
M Scott	S Mitchell
P Turner	M Griffiths
J Huxley	M White
P Rees	D Cronin
P O'Neill	M Greenwood
P Angelsea	L Dallaglio
A Bennett	C Sheasby

Scorers

Orrell. Tries: Lyon, Heslop, Bennett, Naylor. Penalty: Strett. Conversions: Strett (2).

Wasps. Tries: Scrase (2), Roiser (2), Tuigamala, Sheasby. Penalties: Rees (2). Conversions: Rees (4).

Replacements

Orrell: J Huxley replaced by A Macfarlane (63 minutes)
Wasps: C Sheasby replaced by N Hadley (76).

2 Things Start to Slide

2 OCTOBER 1996

Anglo-Welsh Cup: Wasps v. Neath. Cancelled

We had advertised the game in the papers. We had ordered the stands. Programmes had been printed. Everything was going according to plan and then Neath phoned up at the eleventh hour to cancel the game. I think we had spent something in the region of £5,000–£6,000 on marketing and all the other necessities. The team had been picked, training had been done, players were expecting to play and Neath phoned up and said they couldn't put out a front row. What we then needed was a statement from the governing body of the game but no one was prepared to come forward. The people at EPRUC (English Professional Rugby Union Clubs) were on holiday and no one was prepared to make a decision. Wasps said it was disgraceful: if they can't get a front row, why can't they just go and borrow one from another team in Wales, pay them a match fee, and get on with it? It seemed like they didn't fancy travelling up to London. I may be doing Neath a discredit – maybe they did have deep problems – but it was clear then that the body running the competition wasn't capable of making a decision as to what should be done, and so Neath were allowed to set a precedent for other clubs to follow. In fact, West Hartlepool cancelled a league fixture with us for the same reason later on. If clubs are going to behave like that there must be rules and guidelines to establish what clubs

45

can and can't do. If there are no rules and guidelines then people will push it as far as they can go.

6 OCTOBER 1996

Courage League Division One: Gloucester 28 Wasps 23

Gloucester's results hadn't gone well for them so far in the season. But we had lost there before, in the Pilkington Cup quarter final, and we were very aware of the environment – a lot of players have gone there and found it very difficult. Tuigamala had a knee injury and Sheasby had a problem with his back but they both came down to watch which indicates the way the game has changed – if you're injured you still travel with the team, you're a squad player and you watch the game. I think they must have both watched with despair.

Gloucester had decided to experiment with a game on a Sunday and we were given the usual Kingsholm ground welcome by the fans in the Shed. It was an enjoyable game and there were no excuses for our defeat – we just played poorly. Gloucester are not as versatile as other sides in the First Division, but whatever they do, they do very well. Richard Hill, their director, had obviously got them fired up and we – perhaps for the first time – didn't show our usual composure and ability under pressure. I don't find the Kingsholm venue as intimidating as it used to be but you can feel like the ground's falling in and swallowing you up and that makes it hard to get out of difficult situations. Gloucester gained confidence from the noisy partisan crowd, which added to our woe. I don't think the referee, Doug Chapman – with whom I don't see eye to eye – had the best of games either. He sent off Kevin Dunn, our ex-Gloucester player. I felt sorry for Kevin. I wouldn't say he stamped on a player although he gave him a pretty fierce rucking – but that's part and parcel of rugby. The guy was clearly lying over the ball, killing it, and Kevin rucked over him. Kevin is an old Gloucester stalwart, so to get sent off at Kingsholm wasn't a pleasant experience. He had only just come on as a replacement and with his departure went our chances of winning the game. You have to give credit to Gloucester though, they played very well and took their chances. They showed the coolness under pressure that we weren't able to do. Individually we did not perform. As captain I have to take a certain amount of responsibility because it's up to me to make decisions and delegate authority, and then hope that the players make correct decisions, but we all let ourselves down.

It was a big disappointment because this was the last of the league games before the European campaign, and to have been able to put the league to one side and go in there six from six would have been ideal. However, we didn't feel that all the good work done by beating Bath and Leicester consecutively had been undone by losing to Gloucester. We realised that no one was going to go unbeaten in the season and, even at that early stage, Leicester had already lost twice and Bath had also lost. There was talk that if you're going to win the league you're still going to lose four games this season. We weren't totally down but it wasn't exactly the ideal platform from which to step up to European competition.

There were a lot of harsh words spoken by myself and a number of other people in the changing room at Gloucester. But we didn't have the chance to put it right immediately because there wasn't a league game the following week. We were moving on to a whole new competition and a new environment but we knew that when we came back to the league we would still be facing played six, won five, lost one. And that one would still be there. It was annoying. But you can't change a result, and we had to put it to the back of our mind and concentrate on Europe. We were looking forward to the competition, even though it came at a bad time.

Gloucester 28 Wasps 23

Gloucester	Wasps
C Catling	G Rees
A Lumsden	L Scrase

A Saverimutto	N Greenstock
M Roberts	A James
M Lloyd	S Roiser
M Mapletoft	A King
S Hamilton	A Gomarsall
A Windo	D Molloy
P Greening	K Dunn
A Deacon	W Green
R Fidler	D Cronin
D Sims	M Greenwood
P Glanville	M White
N Carter	L Dallaglio
S Devereux	P Scrivener

Scorers
Gloucester. Tries: Saverimutto, Catling. Penalties: Mapletoft (6)
Wasps. Tries: Scrase, Gomarsall. Penalties: Rees (3). Conversions: Rees, King.

Replacements
Gloucester: A Deacon replaced by P Vickery (40 minutes), P Glanville replaced by E Pearce (38).
Wasps: S Roiser replaced by D Macer (66), P Scrivener replaced by R Kinsey (34).

13 OCTOBER 1996

Heineken European Cup: Wasps 24 Cardiff 26

I think everyone considered our group the most difficult, calling it the Pool of Death. Toulouse, the holders, were expected to go a similar distance this time round. Cardiff were the Welsh champions, they possessed a number of Welsh internationals and were the team to beat in Wales. We had probably made a better start than any other side to the English domestic season and were the form side in England. Milan were basically the Italian national side, and would present a tough challenge, and everyone, including us, thought that Munster would make up the numbers. That was perhaps a mistake on our part. We were happy that we were playing Cardiff and Toulouse at home, on paper the two most difficult games.

We were quite optimistic about the European Cup. I had watched the competition the previous year, and had thought that it was a super event. But we all thought that it wouldn't be a proper European competition until English clubs took part. I had always been under the impression that the English club scene was far stronger than the Welsh and was on a par with the French. The competition was a tremendous success because it showed us what our strengths and weaknesses were at a higher level of rugby and it was a step up from most league games. We were confident that we would win at home against Cardiff. They had internationals Emyr Lewis, Hemi Taylor, Derwyn Jones, Jonathan Humphries, Robert Howley (an inspiration to them all season), Jonathan Davies and Mike Hall (who almost signed for Wasps). All of our players missing at Gloucester were back for this game. We played poorly but towards the end of the game, Jonathan Davies let us off the hook by missing some kicks. Howley scored a super try down the blind side, and they were the better side for the majority of the game. We did put a lot of pressure on them but they defended very well. We seemed to come away with no tries, just penalties. We did have a chance to score when Nick Greenstock had an overlap but he kicked instead, and composure under pressure deserted us. It was ironic because, although we played so badly, we were ahead with only one minute to go. We got a penalty and were suddenly winning the game for the first time in the whole match. To have played that badly and be winning was incredible. And then it came down to the last kick. Jonathan Davies kicked off for them and all we had to do was get the ball off the pitch and the referee would have blown the whistle. We caught it, there was a slight confusion and they hit us with the full weight of their pack. They turned us over and Jonathan Davies hit the winning dropped goal. Only Jonathan Davies could have hit that drop; it was wide out on the left – it was a super kick. I think he had been getting a lot of stick from his own teammates and supporters for missing kicks earlier on. But, to his credit, he hit a beautiful dropped goal and won them the game with the last kick of the match – the referee blew the whistle immediately afterwards.

On balance they deserved to win, and we would have considered ourselves very lucky if we had come away with a victory. They were very quick to come out afterwards and tell us how about the strength of Welsh rugby. It was a blow to us because to qualify now was going to be very difficult. It was a home match and should have been a banker. All the doubts were starting to creep in and the critics were starting to hover and say that Wasps were starting to fall apart. Everything that had been positive, everything that had gone well leading up to that game, was now going pear-shaped. No one could quite put their finger on the exact reason why we had let ourselves down in the last two games. All we could do was take the positive things forward. The game showed us that we were going to have to become much more competitive. Perhaps I'm taking things away from Cardiff but we were very critical of our own performance. Cardiff went on to register a very big win over Bath in the semi-finals so we were beaten by a good side, but we considered ourselves worthy of the latter stages of the competition and felt that we had significantly under-achieved.

Wasps 24 Cardiff 26

Wasps	*Cardiff*
J Ufton	J Thomas
P Sampson	S Hill
N Greenstock	M Hall
V Tuigamala	G Jones
L Scrase	N Walker
G Rees	J Davies
A Gomarsall	R Howley
M Griffiths	L Mustoe
S Mitchell	J Humphreys
W Green	D Young
M White	H Taylor

D Cronin	J Wakeford
M Greenwood	D Jones
L Dallaglio	J Ringer
C Sheasby	E Lewis

Scorers
Wasps. Penalties: Rees (8).
Cardiff. Tries: Howley (2), Lewis. Penalty: Davies. Conversion: Davies.
Dropped goals: Davies (2).

Replacements
Wasps: J Ufton temporarily replaced by M Fraser (22–32 minutes), M White temporarily replaced by J Worsley (31–40).
Cardiff: J Ringer replaced by M Bennett (52).

19 OCTOBER 1996

Heineken European Cup: Munster 49 Wasps 22

This was just about the lowest point of the season. My mother's half-Irish, her family come from Cork, so I have a great deal of affection for Ireland but to lose there was disheartening to say the least.

I was looking forward to this fixture because it was an away trip. All the away trips we had been on so far had been just a trip down the M4 to Bath or a little coach journey to Gloucester. It was exciting to go on a trip with all the boys. I had heard about the fantastic atmosphere created at Munster and read about the big wins that Munster had enjoyed, so I knew that it was a tough place to go and play. But I never envisaged it being quite as disastrous as it turned out to be. The game was at Limerick. It's known as Stab City to many people – they certainly stabbed us. The whole thing had a very amateur, surreal feel about it. There wasn't any trumpet blowing like we had in other European matches and they weren't about to roll out the red carpet just because Wasps were coming to town, but they were very welcoming. When you go to Ireland they lull you into a false sense of security – they tap you on the back and say, 'You're Wasps and you're twenty points better than our team; God, you're going to thrash us, go easy on us.' They're so welcoming that you start feeling comfortable, and then it all goes horribly wrong. It did nothing but pour with rain from the minute we got there until the minute we left, and although I didn't anticipate anything else, it didn't help. We hadn't had much rain at home. We had played Cardiff in perfect sunshine and most of the other matches had been on dry hard ground.

We had lost two games on the trot and, if we were to stand any chance of qualifying for Europe, we had to win this time. Our pride had been hurt by successive defeats and this was a chance to atone for individual mistakes that had been of collective significance. As Munster didn't have the same reputation as some of the other sides, we made the fundamental and unforgivable mistake of underestimating them and not giving them the respect that they deserved. They were all amateurs and many people in the Wasps side felt that because we were suddenly professional we would steamroller them. I don't think any of Munster's players were fully paid professionals. I think Irish international Mick Galwey was perhaps their highest-profile player although they had fellow international David Corkery on the blind side and some other very talented players as well. They taught us a lesson – some of our players physically gave up halfway through the game and that is not something I expect from the Wasps team. It was pouring with rain and the atmosphere was a bit like the cauldron at Gloucester. The ground was opening up and we were sinking into it heavily. A packed crowd came out to watch and most of them got soaked. It didn't matter to them; they wanted to see Munster turn Wasps over, and we suddenly found ourselves in quite a hostile atmosphere. We were expecting a tough crowd but you can never quite prepare yourself for it. We had a French referee who, on a day like that, was probably the worst referee you could have asked for – he just let everything go. He wasn't prepared to talk to the captains, he just kept waving away anyone who wanted to talk to him and they just hacked through any ball that went on the floor.

We had discussed how we would counter the aggressive style of the Irish play. We put Mike Griffiths in the team to give us the extra edge that we had lacked in the scrummage and we had Gareth Rees at fly half, but he had perhaps his worst game of the season. We tried to play the game too wide. We really didn't play well at all. No one took responsibility to take the ball forward and people were passing it laterally. In the circumstances this was the worst thing you could do because these guys were going to tackle all day long, run all day long, work hard, forage and really make life awkward. We needed to get the basics right, to take the ball up through the guts of them, driving hard. Instead, we persisted in trying to run the ball in weather which suggested that this was a foolish option. They got a couple of early penalties and a try and we were something like twenty-two points down quite quickly. We never really recovered, even though we did get a try just before half time and a couple of penalties – all of a sudden there was only a score in it. When we started to take the game to them, to drive it hard up the middle and not over-elaborate, things began to work. Then in the second half they came out even stronger, and our players started to miss tackles and look at each other with their hands on their hips. Meanwhile Munster took their opportunities. They played with a passion from which we should have learnt. They played out of their skins and everything we tried went wrong. We were now nearly thirty points down so we had to throw caution to the wind. We played like a side who were desperate to try anything, but nothing came off.

I played as badly as anyone else on the field. It was my worst match as captain. It was one of my worst moments with the Wasps. It's very difficult to motivate your side when they've got forty-four points on the scoreboard. I was just so annoyed and disappointed because I knew our chances of qualifying from the group were gone and that it was a hell of a long journey back. This was our third successive defeat and it was very depressing. I know everyone else felt it as well, but when you're captain of the side you feel it even more because you shoulder the responsibility. It leaves a lot of scars and takes a lot of getting over. It was one of those games where you're just praying for the final whistle to put you out of your misery. And it was all self-made misery. In the changing room afterwards, for the first time I said nothing – I felt I had no right as I had played as badly as anyone else on the field. I didn't have any right to get up and pontificate about spirit and tackling, about doing the basics right and how we should have played because I had let the team, and myself, down. Rob Smith and Nigel Melville absolutely laid into us about our attitude and performance. There was a numb feeling in the dressing room – no one said a word. No one even moved for about ten minutes, we were in such a state of shock. When you win you could have your heart hanging off and you wouldn't notice it but when you lose, and get thoroughly taken to the cleaners, you suffer. There was blood all over the changing room with guys lying there, not only shocked but in a state of disrepair as well. We had gone down heavily casualty-wise and we hadn't even gone down fighting. Although a couple of people came out with their heads held high, I don't include myself as one of them. There were a lot of fingers pointing in a lot of directions and a lot of soul-searching as well. The whole weekend had been a disaster from start to finish.

Munster 49 Wasps 22

Munster	Wasps
P Murray	J Ufton
R Wallace	P Sampson
B Walsh	N Greenstock
S McCahill	V Tuigamala
D Crotty	S Roiser
K Keane	G Rees
S McIvor	A Gomarsall

J Fitzgerald	M Griffiths
T Kingston	S Mitchell
N Healy	W Green
A Foley	M White
M Galwey	D Cronin
G Fulcher	M Greenwood
D Corkery	L Dallaglio
B Cronin	C Sheasby

Scorers
Munster. Tries: Foley, Galwey, Keane, Cronin, Wallace, Crotty, penalty try. Penalties: Keane (2). Conversions: Keane (4).
Wasps. Tries: Sheasby, Green, Greenstock, Roiser. Conversion: Ufton.

Replacement
Wasps: A Gomarsall replaced by M Wood (71 minutes).

I had some friends who had bought a house an hour south of Dublin and so I arranged for them to come and watch. They had driven a long way to see us play, it had poured with rain and we had put on a disastrous performance. It seemed to me that we lost every game that they came to watch. A guy called Barney Cordell had a horse running at Limerick Races on the Sunday and the idea was that they would all come and watch the rugby and I would then watch the races with them the day after, gamble my match fee on a horse called Go Now, and it would be a super day. Accordingly, I had booked my flight back a day later than everyone else. Had we won, I don't think anyone would have made anything of it but because we lost, it was selfish of me to have gone through with it. I should have been with the team at a time when, given my own performance, they needed me there. But I stayed the extra day and went to Limerick Races, trying to make something of a terrible weekend. The horse finished second, it was still pouring with rain and, as I wandered around the racecourse, I was easily recognisable as that English player with his tail between his legs. The racegoers were typically Irish, saying, 'Better luck next time' and 'Don't worry, you're still a good player'. I just couldn't wait to get home. The whole weekend had been planned meticulously and had gone wrong from start to finish.

When I arrived back on the Monday I sat down with Nigel Melville. Clearly things weren't working out too well for the team. Had we won, things would have been overlooked. But we lost, and the manner in which we lost – my performance, and the team's performance – meant that the fact that I had gone missing on Sunday and didn't travel back with the rest of the boys was well noted. What right did I have to stay behind horse racing and gambling in Limerick when things had gone so badly wrong? I congratulated Mick Galwey and his team and I was brutally honest with my own team. I said that we had found out a lot about each other and that it was probably the worst performance I had been involved in since I joined Wasps. We had badly underestimated the strength of Munster and shown them no respect, and they had made us pay dearly for it. As the captain, I needed to be spoken to about my responsibilities. I was made aware that people followed my example and that the one I had set in Ireland was the worst I had set since taking over the captaincy. It made me realise that sometimes you can't take everything for granted – on occasions I have thought that I have the Midas touch and that good things just happen naturally. It's something that, as a captain, you have to work at, and although I've been blessed with some talent I shouldn't take it for granted. My responsibilities were spelt out to me in no uncertain terms by people whom I respect: Nigel Melville and Rob Smith. Then we talked about the team and how we were playing. Clearly, you don't lose three games on the trot if things are going hunky-dory. There was definitely something wrong, not just with the commitment and the attitude – the mental side of the team – but also on the physical, playing side. What had been successful in the opening games was clearly not successful now, and something needed to be done to turn things round immediately. It was urgent because our next game was against Toulouse, possibly the hardest game in the group – they had beaten Cardiff in France quite comfortably. Things were looking ominous. Clubs like Leicester, Bath and Wasps just don't lose three games on the trot. The vultures were circling above our heads and critics began to pick holes in what had looked a very strong and formidable outfit, so we decided to make some changes. The most significant was me moving back to the blind side.

A lot has been made of my positional preferences, and coaches' positional preferences for me. When I first started playing rugby as a back row player I was a No. 8. At school, and when I first joined Wasps as a colt that was my position. It gave me the freedom to rove and range and it fed my strength which is to run at people, ball in hand. I joined Wasps when there was a galaxy of back row players, the talent there was endless – Dean Ryan, who had just been capped by England, Francis Emeruwa, who could have been capped in any of three positions, Buster White, Mark Ellison, Mark Rose and Chris Wilkins. They were not just good players but the very essence of Wasps, the backbone of the club. So to break into the team was very difficult and with a personality like Dean Ryan at No. 8 it was going to be hard to get in there, so I started playing No. 6. Rob Andrew eventually said that they had to find a place for me in the team because I could give an attacking option that they hadn't had for some while, and Dean felt that I was always a bit loose as a player and so they could safely stick me at No. 6. Dean said, 'You'll have to start making some tackles and getting involved. You'll get trodden on and kicked to pieces for a while but let's see how you like it.' So I played No. 6 and thoroughly enjoyed it. Then I had a brief flirtation with No. 7 at the beginning of the 1994–95 season – in fact, I made my debut against Harlequins at No. 7. It went OK; people said that I might be one to watch in the future and we won. We then had Newcastle Gosforth at home and beat them as well. Then we went to Leicester away where I played against Neil Back.

I'd become ill that week (I had flu) and should have pulled

out but because it was only my third first team game I wasn't thinking sensibly. I had to stay in the team and if I pulled out and someone else had a good game I would lose my place, so I played and we were soundly beaten. I was totally ineffective because I was mentally and physically drained by the illness; I was beaten to every breakdown and I missed tackles. We lost 38–3, a record margin against Leicester. I was dropped after that game and didn't really feature for the rest of the season. I made the odd appearance on the wing as a replacement for speed merchant Chris Oti, which seemed to be quite a regular thing. It was nice that they had the confidence to stick me on the wing instead of putting a winger in there but I was still desperately disappointed. I then came back as a No. 6 and really enjoyed playing blind side – I believe I could have played any of the three back row positions. If I had stuck with open side I could have been good, but I was happy to play No. 6 and that's where I have stayed ever since really, until Jack Rowell decided to move me to No. 7 for England. It was almost a relief when Nigel Melville asked me what I felt was my best position. I told him that it was either No. 6 or No. 8, but not No. 7.

Something was clearly going wrong on the playing side. The continuity wasn't there and there was a confusion between roles – decisions would have to be made. We started talking about the Toulouse game and what we were going to do to win. It wasn't a particularly long meeting but the decision was made that I should revert to No. 6. The line-out wasn't functioning well either. I had always been a part of the line-out, and if I was at No. 6 I was going to be so much more involved in the physical side of the game. I had felt lost playing at No. 7, and that I couldn't make a physical statement there. If you're chasing a kickoff at No. 6 you're in the game immediately, you're making tackles – you're able to get into the game far quicker than you can at No. 7. That was what I enjoyed doing and when I was getting the ball at No. 7 I was giving it away again, and that wasn't playing to my strengths.

Players in this country don't seem to possess the same explosive power that they possess down under, so guys tend to go to the floor very quickly here. This means that as an open sider you're invariably the first one to arrive at a breakdown and if someone's gone to the floor it's a very messy situation. I would end up tied in at the bottom of a pile-up, having secured the ball and given it away to someone but I was then effectively out of the game. It was like carrying a ball and chain because I wasn't enjoying it. I felt that my strengths as a rugby player lay in running at defences, drawing in defenders and creating overlaps – which is best achieved by arriving second and third at the breakdown because I could then read the situation. It's better in the southern hemisphere because when you arrive at a breakdown the players are still on their feet. They unload the ball either before contact or in contact, and the game seems to have a lot more continuity. Guys tend to go to ground as soon as they get tackled over here. The defence try to get their hands on the ball and slow it up and kill it, and it makes it very difficult to achieve the continuity you find down under.

I knew the positional switch would create pressure. People would start asking questions, people would start noticing. It was close to the announcement of the England selection as well. There was speculation about who was going to be picked, and I know selector Don Rutherford had come to watch a number of our games. If I hadn't been captain I wouldn't have been surprised if I had been dropped from the Wasps team after our poor run, but we decided to make only minor adjustments. Sampson came back on the right wing, I went to No. 6, Buster White went back to No. 7, Molloy came on at loose head, Alex King went to fly half and Gareth Rees moved to fullback. Rees had his worst game of the season at fly half against Munster. His performance, given the amount of test experience he has had playing for Canada, was disappointing for us and for him. The one thing about Wasps has always been that there's a pride in winning, and to lose three consecutive games is unheard of at the club. Everyone was well aware of the significance of losing another match and well aware that, even though qualification for Europe had now perhaps slipped away, the importance of a strong performance against Toulouse could not be underestimated. We needed it to rebuild the confidence of the team and to re-establish what had been so successful in the opening few games of the season.

26 OCTOBER 1996

Heineken European Cup: Wasps 77 Toulouse 17

The build-up to the Toulouse game was unusual because their fly half, Thomas Castaignede, was spouting off in the papers about English rugby, saying that we only knew how to play one way – killing the ball and slowing the game up. I don't know how many players picked up on it but I certainly noticed it, and it particularly annoyed me because it wasn't true at all. Look at the way France played against us in the Five Nations, when he kicked that winning dropped goal – I don't think he had any grounds to suggest that we were the only side that played that way. I think Toulouse made the same mistake with us that we had made with Munster. They underestimated us, and didn't pay enough attention to what goes on in league rugby in England. They weren't even aware that we were top of the league. I think they play with a certain arrogance and confidence which means that when things go well they go very well, and they become a beautiful team to watch.

But on this occasion they came over and showed us no respect. They were full of international stars: Ntamack, Califano, Castaignede, etc. We were fully aware of their capabilities but they had no idea against whom they were playing. I imagine the only footage they saw was our performance against Cardiff, and since they beat Cardiff very comfortably, they were obviously very confident about their chances of success against us. Over-confident probably. I know from my experience of playing French sides that they don't travel well, whoever they are.

Nigel Melville made it clear what was to be achieved out there, and how important the fixture was in re-establishing our status within the game. This was going out live on French and South African TV. ITV had given up their proposed coverage so no one outside the ground was really watching the game in Britain. I have never seen us as focused as we were for that game. Against Munster everything we tried went wrong; against Toulouse everything we tried went right. You couldn't have asked for a better performance, and it was a shame it wasn't televised in Britain because, along with Leicester against Toulouse and Brive against Leicester, it was one of the best rugby matches of the season. I think the French were blown away because we played the sort of rugby that they aspire to play in France. Toulouse are the Manchester United of French rugby. The other French teams are envious of Toulouse's success, and so our victory over them went down very well in some parts of France. Everyone had been waiting for it to happen.

The Toulouse coach was very complimentary about Wasps. He said he hadn't realised there were players in this country who could play like that and that we had played a superb match. We did really. We once counter-attacked from behind our own goal line with Alex King starting and Nick Greenstock finishing the ball; it went through about eight or nine pairs of hands, the whole length of the pitch. We scored nine tries and won by sixty points, a huge margin. It was significant enough to make everyone take note that Wasps had got their house back in order. And it was a massive turn around.

Wasps 77 Toulouse 17

Wasps	*Toulouse*
J Ufton	S Ougier
P Sampson	E Ntamack

Diary of a Season

N Greenstock	M Marfaing
V Tuigamala	T Castaignede
S Roiser	D Berty
A King	C Deylaud
A Gomarsall	J Tilloles
D Molloy	C Califano
S Mitchell	D Guiter
W Green	J-L Jordana
L Dallaglio	J-L Cester
D Cronin	H Miorin
A Reed	F Belot
M White	H Manent
C Sheasby	S Dispagne

Scorers
Wasps. Tries: Greenstock (2), Reed, Roiser, Mitchell, Sampson, Sheasby, King, penalty try. Penalties: Ufton (6). Conversions: Ufton (6).
Toulouse. Tries: Ntamack, Lasserre. Penalty: Castaignede. Conversions: Deylaud (2).

Replacements
Wasps: D Cronin replaced by M Greenwood (65 minutes), D Molloy replaced by I Dunston (74), P Sampson replaced by L Scrase (75), W Green replaced by D Macer (76).
Toulouse: T Castaignede replaced by O Carbonneau (23), D Guiter replaced by P Lasserre (40), D Berty replaced by X Garbajosa (44), J-L Cester replaced by D Lacroix (54), S Ougier replaced by F Cazaux (63).

A French friend of mine, Jean Philippe, who runs a restaurant in Kingston and has been a Wasps supporter ever since I met him last year brought his son along for the game. He asked me to get a Toulouse shirt signed for him before the match. He gave me the shirt – he likes to put all the shirts up in the restaurant – and a gold pen and asked me to get the Toulouse team to sign it. So, before the game I went to our manager, Malcolm Sinclair, gave him the shirt and asked if he would take it into their dressing room and get their players to sign it. He came back before kickoff and said they told him to f*** off. In French. After the game he asked me if I wanted him to take it in there again, but I said that I didn't think that it would be a good idea. I didn't think they would particularly want anyone in their dressing room then. So I took the shirt back upstairs to Jean Philippe and apologised that I hadn't been able to get any signatures. He took the shirt back. He had his arm in a tricolor-decorated plaster and beneath his Wasps shirt he wore a French shirt. He went looking for the Toulouse players and found them all outside the stadium, eating their meal on some steps. They were all hanging their heads in shame. He took his Wasps shirt off and he took his Toulouse shirt up to them and asked for their signatures. He said to them something like, 'Come on lads, it's not the end of the world, I'm French, you're French and let's celebrate that.' I think they were so delighted to see one of their own that he got his shirt signed. Then he put his Wasps shirt back on and came running upstairs – he was absolutely delighted. We proceeded to buy a few bottles of Chablis and celebrate accordingly.

It had been a fantastic team performance and clearly we had had an incredible revival. The whole team played very well and it got us right back on track. We had learnt some hard lessons from our involvement in Europe but we showed that, on our day, we are capable of beating any side in the northern hemisphere.

The people who were there were privileged to witness a super game of rugby. I was the first one to send that tape up to Leicester and Bob Dwyer when I realised Toulouse were playing Leicester in the semi finals. The one thing that stuck out a mile was the fact that Toulouse were trying to play rugby all the way through the game. They weren't killing ball, which perhaps explains the scoreline. They followed the same philosophy as they follow in the southern hemisphere – as soon as one of our players had gone into contact, gone down, turned the right way and secured the ball for our side, they didn't put their hands on it or lie over it; they didn't try to kill the ball. I don't think that's in their nature. I think that was why we were able to have a game like that. It just so happened that, on the day, we played the better attacking rugby. We defended well and forced them into making mistakes, and every time we got an opportunity we took it and scored. But, compared to other sides, it just struck me that their attitude towards the game was very positive.

A lot of people have pointed towards the southern hemisphere and said that the Super 12 competition isn't as good as we think it is. I don't necessarily believe that but I think there are two fundamental differences between the two styles of rugby. Firstly, when a law is passed over there, the referees referee that law straight away and players are told in no uncertain terms that any overstep of the mark will result in a penalty. Take the law change about binding on the back row for instance. The referees in the southern hemisphere stressed that law to such an extent that everyone in the back row now binds on the scrummage whereas over here, people are cheating by popping their heads up. The No. 8 law has also changed. Now the No. 8 has to stay in the No. 8 slot and the southern hemisphere referees, but not the referees here, are applying the rule rigidly.

The other difference concerns the players' attitudes. Over there, as soon as a guy goes into a tackle and turns the right way, there are two of his team mates supporting him to make sure he's secured the ball. One tackler goes in, two guys make sure someone doesn't drive through the middle and everyone else is spread across the pitch. In other words, they're not trying to get their hands on the ball, they're not chasing lost causes. All you hear the referee saying is 'Leave it alone, leave it alone,' and the players get on with it. Over here, as soon as a player has turned, the usual attitude is to get hands on the ball, to try and nick it back, or to try and slow it down. They're not thinking about trying to defend it again, only about slowing the ball down.

Until these two fundamental areas are changed, I don't think we're going to get games of equivalent excitement or skill. People talk about game plans but it's the attitude of players and the way that attitude is assisted by the referee which is going to change the game over here. That's why I thought it would be interesting to see the meeting of these two styles in the British Lions' tour, to see what the spin-off would be. I believed that unless we adopted a similar style then there was a danger of us struggling against the South Africans.

3 International Calls

2 NOVEMBER 1996

Heineken European Cup: Milan 23 Wasps 33

Milan was a very significant fixture for me because of my previous flirtation with the possibility of going to play rugby there. I first played for England Under 19s, the England Colts, against Italy Colts at Grange Road, Cambridge University. I was playing No. 8. The Italians saw my name in the programme and thought that this guy must be an Italian; what's he doing playing for England? My father, a full Italian, was there and a few discussions followed. A letter arrived from an Italian club called Rovigo, and then another from Milan suggesting they would like to arrange a meeting in Italy. I was eighteen years old, and it was a wonderful opportunity. I was cautious, and thankful I had my father with me. Just before I was to go to university at Kingston, we flew to Italy to watch a club match. My eyes were opened out there. We had been talking about the game being amateur as Italy had only been playing rugby seriously for a very short time but they were as professional as anyone I have seen in the new era. The whole English concept of playing a game of rugby and going out and getting stoned on twenty pints doesn't exist in Italy, it's not in their make up. We were put up in a superb hotel and taken to watch Milan play L'Aquila. David Campese was playing at full back. Unfortunately, the standard of rugby was as poor as the refereeing. Poor Campese was so frustrated it was unbelievable – he gets frustrated by top class refereeing let alone dodgy Italian referees. The players with skill and commitment stood out a mile, but they were few and far between. Milan had been champions for the past few years and the only club side who had got anywhere near them was Treviso, where Michael Lynagh was playing at the time. The lifestyle seemed superb. I watched the game and then met the players in the changing room. Afterwards we all went into Milan, to a big restaurant where we sat down as a family, rather than a team. We had the meal which, in typical Italian style, went on for about four or five hours; course after course of beautiful food, served with lovely wine. Already it was becoming very tempting.

They had obviously done their homework on me and saw that the way to attract me was through my stomach, and a couple of bottles of decent red wine. I couldn't help but notice when it came to paying that both Mark Ella and David Campese had pretty impressive credit cards in their wallets. Perhaps other people wouldn't have noticed but my eyes tended to wander all over the place that night. I never stopped looking and learning. Campese was very open and honest, saying, 'Get yourself out here, the rugby's great and you'll probably earn as much money as I can.' He obviously didn't realise how young I was or that I was a totally unknown rugby player who had played no club rugby back in England of any distinction, and had played only one game for England Colts against Italy. Campese had already won 60 caps and was now having a great time earning a quarter of a million dollars in Milan. I think he worked as a PA for a golf club part time, and played rugby the rest of the time. It showed me what opportunities there were in Italian rugby. There is a complex in Milan built by media mogul Silvio Berlusconi, called Milano Due (Milan 2) which is a bit like Loughborough University – a huge sports complex. He owned the rugby team, the football team, the basketball team, the water polo team and other sports teams to boot.

Apart from the football players, who were on a different planet, all the other sportspeople lived on this complex. Each player had a nice two-bedroom flat within the complex, with all expenses paid, and the facilities available were just superb. If you were into fitness and sport, you couldn't ask for a better environment – swimming pools, restaurants, tennis courts, running tracks and a weights room the size of anyone else's gymnasium, all on your doorstep. The ski slopes were an hour and a half away. This was where I would live. I could go skiing in the Dolomites and be near Milan, the centre of the fashion industry. I spoke reasonable Italian, and they were offering me a place at Milan university, one of the best in Italy. Plus they would have paid me at a time when clearly that was not allowed in Britain. The concept of not paying a player for his services was unheard of there. They were investing heavily in rugby and they saw that by bringing over people like Campese and Lynagh that, although in the short term it would cost them a lot of money, in the long term it would bring valuable publicity to the game there. Trying to compete with football wasn't even worth considering, but they thought that rugby could still thrive. They had come on so much in a relatively short period of time, an indication of how much they were prepared to invest at grass roots level. Milan are a good side now and there is talk of Italy being in the Five Nations, yet it was only in 1991 that I was over there watching a very average club game. In six years, they've come on tremendously.

It was a huge temptation. I went home and considered it and thought it would be lovely: I would have a huge flat, play rugby and study at university in Milan. Fortunately, I had my dad, and because of his knowledge of Italy, we were able to paint a much wider picture than just that of an English family going over there to live. We all travelled home after a lovely weekend away and discussed this wonderful offer. I have a great deal of affection for Italy, and there is a certain amount of Italian culture ingrained in me, but I was born in Shepherds Bush and, although we used to go on holiday to Italy and I spoke a bit of Italian I just felt like a very English person. I had now had a taste of playing rugby for England, and I really enjoyed the feeling of putting on the red rose and white shirt of England – it was a great buzz. And I knew what rugby meant to the people in England compared to what it meant in Italy. For that reason alone, I had already decided that my ambition was to play for England. There was now a definite structure in place where guys who had played for England at a lower level were likely to go on to play at a higher level. Nobody was fast-tracked though – we still don't do that as quickly as we should, but certainly there was a ladder in place, and if you had the skill, determination and dedication, you could climb up that ladder and go on to play for England. Had the Italian offer come before I represented England, I would probably have accepted it. All the reservations and hesitations that my father had about my education were put to bed by the fact that they offered me a place at university. In Italy they were very keen to see professional sportsmen proactive in either employment or study, and they monitored players very closely to see what they did off the pitch. This is something which is perhaps overlooked in this country, but certainly wasn't overlooked in Italy. My father didn't have any hesitations about it, and I think, had I decided to go there, the whole family might have moved. My sister was involved in professional dancing, so she could travel all over the world. But I had already had a taste of playing for England, I was really enjoying things at Wasps and I had just accepted a place at Kingston University.

Looking at the Milan fixture triggered all these memories. I had never envisaged Milan playing the likes of Wasps, not so soon anyway. I never envisaged Italy doing particularly well at international level. They wanted me over there because I had dual nationality and so could have played for Italy in the last World Cup. I would probably have had fifty

Italian caps by now. The prospect of playing a rugby match in Italy was, therefore, intriguing. There was no pressure on us because we couldn't qualify. We just had to finish with a good performance. And it would be a chance to get an away trip going with a bit of team spirit.

The stadium took you back to Roman times, to what could possibly have gone on there. There were cages underneath the ground and you couldn't help thinking that there must be dungeons somewhere around. There were only about 1,000 people watching the match in a stadium which probably held about 65,000, which was a shame. But we still enjoyed it. It was a useful lesson for Gomarsall, Sheasby and myself because later we were to be picked for the England team that played Italy. Bath were playing Treviso the same weekend and between the two of us we came back with a wealth of information on the Italian team. We certainly learned a lot about Diego Dominguez – a world class goal kicker. We played reasonably well and Alex King hit a dropped goal which eventually put us out of sight, but they gave us a tough game which we thoroughly enjoyed.

Milan 23 Wasps 33

Milan	*Wasps*
M Bonomi	J Ufton
N Scanziani	P Sampson
A Stoica	N Greenstock
M Tomazzi	V Tuigamala
Marcello Cuttitta	S Roiser
D Dominguez	A King
F Gomez	A Gomarsall
Massimo Cuttita	D Molloy
A Marengoni	D Macer
F Properzi	I Dunston
P Pedroni	M Greenwood
G Croci	A Reed
C Orlandi	L Dallaglio
D Beretta	M White
O Arancio	C Sheasby

Diary of a Season

Scorers
Milan. Tries: Gomez, Marcello Cuttitta. Penalties: Dominguez (3).
Conversions: Dominguez (2).
Wasps. Tries: Sampson (2), Dallaglio, King. Penalties: Ufton (2).
Conversions: Ufton (2). Dropped goal: King.

Replacements
Milan: C Orlandi replaced by S Tassi (50).
Wasps: A Gomarsall replaced by M Wood (79).

I roomed with Inga for the first time that weekend. We went into the room and had the double bed/single bed scenario, and he said, 'You have the double bed,' and I said, 'No you have it, honestly.' He read the Bible while I read a diary of Alec Guinness's. He read some of the parables to me. I think he thought he might make an impression on me; I don't think he realised I'd had four or five years of Catholicism at Ampleforth School surrounded by monks. We had a long chat about his past and his aspirations for the future. We just talked about families – his wife was expecting another child, and Alice, my girlfriend, was expecting our child. I thought I'd keep that under wraps. You could have told Inga anything and if you'd said don't tell anyone he wouldn't have done, but I felt at the time it wasn't appropriate and I thought he might make an issue of the fact that I wasn't married. So I kept my mouth shut, and we got on very well and had a good time.

It was a bank holiday in Italy at the time, so Milan was very quiet. I think a lot of the guys were expecting a hub of excitement with bars, shops and models everywhere. It's not really like that even in normal times – you have to be in the know to find it. So we ended up being very low-key. We had the team together after the game for the usual Italian buffet. It was a lovely evening in Milan and we came back to the hotel together, had a good few drinks and a bit of fun and games. And then everyone went off in their own directions. I went out for a few drinks with some of the younger players. And there was quite a bit of Wasps support out there. The whole weekend had been quite a success. We had won. We obviously hadn't reached the same heady heights as we had against Toulouse the week before but we'd had a thoroughly enjoyable game and we could now go back to begin the second wave of league rugby with renewed enthusiasm. We had recaptured and rekindled some of the form that had lit up the beginning of the season.

Europe was disappointing in that people's expectations from the group were that it would probably be between Wasps, Cardiff and Toulouse, but it happened to be Cardiff and Toulouse, not Wasps. There was definitely room for improvement – it was essential if we were to compete, both domestically and in Europe. Hopefully, the lessons have been learnt. From my point of view, the experience came and went very quickly.

The captaincy of England had already been decided before we flew home. However, it was not just the captaincy that was being talked about – the game had now been declared professional for 1996–97. The talk and the bar banter switched from captaincy to contracts, from clubs to money, and there was a tremendous amount of panic. Uncertainty revolved around the structure of the game, and who controlled that structure. Cliff Brittle had been named chairman of the RFU and he said that he was going to stand for everything that rugby was about. The RFU were suggesting that the game would always be run by them and that there was no other way the game could go forward. The players just got on with the playing. We felt they were being put in a very delicate situation and when you have to dodge political questions such as 'which England team do you want to play for if there is a split?' you do not want to alienate yourself from anyone. We wanted some sort of clear direction, we just needed to see some sort of agreement made. There was also a tremendous amount of excitement, and I thought throughout the summer that all these arguments would be thrashed out and we would arrive at the start of the season with a clear mission statement from the RFU. The players could then really get on with the playing.

From the start, there was a difference of opinion between the RFU and the players, although the players weren't really that involved at this stage. People couldn't agree on most issues: control, money, who should play, whether we should be playing clubs, whether we should be playing divisional rugby, whether we should be playing European rugby, how many competitions there should be, who should control the split of money, etc. There's no wonder there were differences of opinion because there was so much to discuss. RUPA (the Rugby Union Players' Association) was formed by Richard Moon, and he put together an objective and a mission statement. As a first division club, we felt that RUPA was a good idea. But I felt that it was representative of everyone who played rugby, from grass roots level up, and the issues raised concerned only the top four divisions, not the whole game. We had to become a bit more specific and therefore we looked at setting up an association of First Division players which ended up covering the top two divisions. We had a meeting with RUPA where we tried to get all the First Division captains to Leamington Spa towards the end of April 1996. It was becoming more difficult to get all twelve captains under one roof so we broke that down to having a steering committee to take our views forward. We could get a hard-core group together, best represented by splitting geographically and we looked at how players were going to be contracted, the pros and cons of one model contract for every player and so on. Then we started meeting with EPRUC.

We started meeting with the RFU as it became clear that the EPRUC agenda and structural view of the future was very different to that of the RFU. The talks concluded in May but the players had to rely on the media for information – we didn't really know what was going on. It was a very unsatisfactory state of affairs but the players took the view that something would be sorted out before the season started. However, the question of control, and of the structure for the future remained a huge talking point. It was just a shame that the talking points in the papers and in the bar after the game were not about the rugby on the pitch but about all these side issues.

All the players had accepted contracts with their clubs and not the RFU. This meant that the England squad were now out of contract with the RFU. Legally, there was only one place that loyalty could lie – to the club. The contract did actually specify some sort of release for England duty; the clubs were not saying that we could no longer play international rugby. I don't think that any player would have signed that sort of contract. At this point there was a breakdown in negotiations and, as a result, EPRUC announced that the clubs were going to withdraw from the union. They asked the players to go to an emergency meeting and said that the possibility of a breakaway was on the cards. At the meeting they put forward the point of view that we were in a no-win situation and the only way it could be sorted out was by giving them our support.

We came out of that meeting firmly behind the clubs. It was solid. At the end of the day club rugby is a player's lifeline, it is what gets him selected for England and not the other way round; it's your bread and butter, and even more so now. But no one would be railroaded into making decisions and I think all decisions that were taken at club level showed that the relationship between the club and players remained strong. By the end of the meeting it was fairly clear that the players fully supported the ideas put forward by EPRUC.

The England captaincy had been a talking point from the beginning of the season and, as a candidate, I was obviously very excited. It was kind of Jack Rowell to warn me that I was not his choice before he named Phil de Glanville at Twickenham. Jack phoned me up as I was driving to training. To be able to turn up at the club and be surrounded by mates at that time was great. The build-up to the announcement had gone on for nine months, since Will Carling made his decision to step down. When I arrived at the club I told Nigel Melville, Roger Uttley and Rob Smith but decided not to tell too many of the players because I didn't want to distract their focus. They would find out in the papers tomorrow anyway. I trained that night and although I wouldn't say it was the best training session I had ever done it certainly helped to put the disappointment out of my mind. I phoned Alice who was new to the rugby environment; she was very encouraging and very supportive, but also very relieved.

I then phoned Jason Leonard, another candidate for the captaincy, who had just finished training at Harlequins. We decided to get together for a beer and ended up going to the fish restaurant in Kingston. Jason was taking his French players there to give them a bit of a taste of home. So he went to the restaurant with Laurent Cabannes and Laurent Benezech and I met them there. What was only supposed to be a couple of quiet drinks and a chat about what had happened ended up finishing at about 3 a.m. after several bottles of beer, red wine and champagne. I had not spoken to Laurent Cabannes much in the past. I had certainly never sat down and had a proper meal with him and we got on really well. He's a lovely guy, a well respected player and great fun on a night out.

We surrounded ourselves with a few comforts – good food, good wine and good company. Jason and I had a good chat and laughed and joked about what would have happened if one of us had been captain and how long it would have taken the tabloids to have responded to our captaincy. Jason is obviously a square-shouldered bloke and I assumed he had been coping with the pressure of the build-up quite well. It was not until I saw him that night that I realised that perhaps he had been in the same sort of fraught position as me. We were two peas in the same pod. I feel that when you do have setbacks and you are disappointed, instead of showing them emotionally in the first instance, you tend to retreat into yourself and lick your wounds. But when you resurface you are stronger, much more ready for anything, and a lot wiser. I think that was the case for both of us.

Jack Rowell never mentioned to me that he had made Phil de Glanville captain but when Jason told me that it wasn't him either, the two of us were pretty clear as to what decision had been made. The thing that annoyed me was that right up until the bookies had closed Phil would have been 25–1 and it had been a little bit naïve of me to think that it was a two-horse race and that the outsider wouldn't win. It rather annoyed me that I never had a bet. I should have had a flutter. Jason and I were laughing about the fact that we should have had a few quid on Phil.

James Grant, my agents, look after Phil as well. They were disappointed on the one hand, but delighted on the other: it was a no-lose situation for them, but as much as they were delighted for Phil they were genuinely disappointed for me. They probably felt that I needed a shoulder to cry on. I went out for a beer with my friends Pete, Russ and Ashley. Just as we were going, the phone rang. It was Phil, saying that I must be disappointed. I said, 'Look mate, at the end of the day you have got the job and I am very pleased for you. The best thing I can do is to make sure that I am playing well and that I am as helpful as possible. I will give you my full support and if there is anything that I can do as a club captain, player or an England teammate then I will be only too willing to do so.' I genuinely meant that. I have a lot of respect for Phil as a player and a captain and I knew it would be a difficult time for him because of the glare of the media spotlight. He needs people who can be positive around him, on and off the field. It was good to speak to him at that stage, and I congratulated him. We were training the next day for England, and a new era was just beginning.

The spotlight was on Phil but obviously people also wanted to gauge my reaction to what had happened. I said that we could look forward to a new era, to Phil leading us out and making sure that we are as successful, if not more successful, than the England team that Will Carling captained. We had a chance to go forward. I think that the most important thing was to focus on the first game against Italy.

6 NOVEMBER 1996

Anglo-Welsh Cup: Pontypridd 19 Wasps 29

This game came at the right time – after we had done so badly in Europe. We had got back on track by playing well against Toulouse but we needed to maintain form for the London Irish game in the league. We needed a big confidence booster against Pontypridd. We had a good result, scoring three tries and really enjoying ourselves. Gomarsall and Sheasby had just heard that they had won their first England caps and they were on the phone nonstop. Gomarsall was driving and Sheasby was in the back – it was like a BT phone exchange. It was unbelievable the amount of calls they made. They were both excited and I was tremendously pleased for them but I also tried to remind them that a cap counts for nothing when you get down to Wales. So I had a smile when we paid the toll and got over the Severn bridge and the reception on the mobile went a bit crackly.

I was delighted for them because on their early season form no one deserved it more than those two, and also Alex King was on the bench. It gave everyone at the club a buzz. Wasps have never really had more than two people involved in England at any one time over the past decade. Rob Andrew and Jeff Probyn were regulars, but there were never more than that. Now, here we were with four people out of twenty-one in the match squad – a big statement about the progress Wasps had made. Players were being picked on form as opposed to reputation. Sheasby deserved to have been picked the year before. For players at Wasps it showed that for a lot of hard work and commitment there was a possibility of recognition. The game against Pontypridd became almost a celebration of that fact.

16 NOVEMBER 1996

Courage League Division One: London Irish 20 Wasps 22

This game preceded the international against Italy. The tradition has always been that anyone who gets a new cap is rested the week prior to an international. But this was a chance for us to assert some authority in the league and therefore Gomarsall and Sheasby were still selected to play. Gomarsall had not wanted to play – you could see that by his performance. He had worked so hard to get international recognition and did not want to get injured. He didn't show the same sort of authority that he had shown in earlier games. Sheasby was much the same, instead of making runs he gave the ball on to someone else. It makes it difficult when confidence and cohesion are lacking at No. 8 and No. 9, and it has a knock-on effect. We were leading 22–3 at half time and we ended up just holding on to win the game 22–20. It was an absolutely phenomenal comeback on their part and the player that stuck out for them was Rob Henderson who had a super game at centre. I think that performance probably made Nigel Melville dip into the transfer market for him when we lost Tuigamala. Every team hits a bad patch somewhere during the season and we were hoping that ours had come over those European games and now gone for good. We had come out the other side but were still not quite reaching the same levels that we had achieved earlier on in the season. On the one hand this result was a little bit worrying, but on the other hand we were still up there at the top – we had never gone seven games in the league with only one defeat before so that was pleasing.

London Irish 20 Wasps 22

London Irish	*Wasps*
C O'Shea	J Ufton
D Charles	P Sampson

R Henderson

J Bishop

N Woods

D Humphreys

P Richards

L Mooney

R Kellam

G Halpin

K O'Connell

J Davidson

M O'Kelly

K Dawson

V Costello

N Greenstock

V Tuigamala

L Scrase

G Rees

A Gomarsall

M Griffiths

S Mitchell

W Green

M White

D Cronin

M Greenwood

L Dallaglio

C Sheasby

Scorers

London Irish. Try: Richards. Penalties: Humphreys (4). Dropped goal: Humphreys.

Wasps. Tries: Sampson, Roiser, Dallaglio. Penalty: Ufton. Conversions: Ufton (2).

23 NOVEMBER 1996

International Match: England 54 Italy 21

The squad assembled at the Compleat Angler Hotel, Marlow, and trained at Bisham. There were some new faces around – Tim Stimpson, Newcastle's fullback, Bath's flying wing, Adedayo Adebayo, a new captain in Phil de Glanville – and some new expectations. It was a new era and so there was a genuine feel-good factor about the team. Shaw was there, Greening was on the bench and King was there, so the average age had gone way down, and that had created a very different atmosphere. There was a genuine buzz about the squad.

I was looking forward to this match tremendously because of my Italian connections and I was really hoping that I would be selected. You hope to be selected for every England game but it was a particularly nice one for me to kick off with. Italy had put together some pretty good performances: they gave Australia a pretty rough ride, they played very well to beat Scotland A (almost a Scotland team) and they should have beaten Wales in Rome where they were very unlucky to have a couple of tries disallowed. They were showing signs of being perfectly capable of competing with the best and I don't think anyone was underestimating the challenge.

We were perfectly aware we needed to put in some good performances in the three games pre-Christmas because it would stand us in good stead for the Five Nations' Championship. So it was very important that we performed. As this was the first rugby international to be played in a professional capacity in Britain there was a lot of speculation and expectation surrounding the game. The selectors were now picking players on form and they seemed to be looking to the future a lot more than they had ever done. We were clearly building for the ultimate prize – the World Cup.

As a captain, Phil de Glanville delegates responsibility very effectively. Players feel able to express themselves individually, to read the game for themselves, to make their own decisions and so to contribute to the team. Players are selected because of their club form but the trick is for them to express themselves in internationals as they would for their club. Phil's captaincy was in a very embryonic stage but it does take time to produce a style. I know that from my experiences as a club captain: you are learning all the time, about the individual personalities in the team and about how best they can gel together and become united. I think Phil was finding his feet, but the important thing was that he had the respect of the players.

This was an ideal game to take over the captaincy. You couldn't ask for a smoother entry into the arena, unlike Carling who started off against Australia. It was also the right time to make changes and pick new caps. We had made five in total: Adebayo, Shaw, Gomarsall, Sheasby and Stimpson. If you are going to make changes, the first international of the season is the time. The changes signalled a clear intent on the part of the selectors as they were to the spine of the team, positions 2, 8, 9, 10 and 15. I think the new players felt surrounded by so much experience and respect that they couldn't fail to perform well. Bristol's Simon Shaw was already a great player and would have been picked for England before had he not suffered from injury problems. I have grown up with Adebayo and I always felt that he consistently performed well year after year at club level for Bath. There were always question marks over his attitude, but no one deserved to get picked more than he did. He is one of the hardest tacklers in the game and having come on as a replacement for Wasps on the wing against Bath I know all about that. I had played with Tim Stimpson at England under-21 level and been on tour to Australia with him. He was always earmarked as a player for the future. Everyone who was picked thoroughly deserved their opportunity.

We were desperate to get going and start playing. We analysed Italy's strengths and weaknesses. There was a lot of video analysis – we looked at their performances against Australia, Wales and Scotland in every detail. We really did our homework and it taught us that if they picked their best fifteen players they were capable of taking on any side. We felt their main strength was their ability to slow the game down effectively. Their players were very streetwise in the tackle and seemed to frustrate the opposition quite easily. They had a very good half-back partnership in Troncon and Dominguez. As a lot of their players are Argentinian or Australian and they have a French coach their game was an amalgam of styles. Their learning experience in rugby has come from the likes of Campese and Lynagh so their education has been a good one. They posed a good threat to us and, to demonstrate their confidence they had been shouting from the roof tops that they should be recognised as a major force in rugby. They wanted to be included in the Five Nations' Championship and there was no better platform to demonstrate their point than in the home of rugby, Twickenham. They could beat Scotland A, they could beat Wales, but they really needed to demonstrate the strength they possessed on a very public stage like Twickenham. They certainly weren't going to come to Twickenham short of motivation. But we were very confident in our own ability; it seemed to me that we really had a good pack now, one that could take on anyone in the world. I am 6ft 4ins and sixteen and a half stone but I am one of the lightest in a well-built but mobile England pack. Shaw was going to fit in very naturally, and he brought the physical presence that England had needed since Wade Dooley retired. Shaw is 6ft 9ins and nearly twenty-one stone, an awesome physical presence in the second row.

The build-up took a very simple course; we spent the beginning of the week looking at them and felt confident that we had the necessary fire power to take them on. They were dealt a massive blow by injury problems, and that ruled out any chance of them gaining an advantage in the set piece area. It was this that denied them possession and cost them the game. The fact that they were effectively without their favoured second row meant that not only could they not win any of our ball, neither could they win any of their own. That set the pattern of the game and effectively ruined the contest.

Italy came over with high hopes and were crushed. They gave away a succession of penalties which put paid to any chance of them making it a competitive match. We were especially pleased with our performance, and it was nice for the five players who came in to start with a good win, but we had not really learnt a great deal. We weren't tested in as many areas as we would have liked to have been and the tries we scored were often off first-phase and second-phase balls. We weren't able to put a number of phases together, something which would be crucial when we played New Zealand and indeed, in the Five Nations'. Scoring over fifty points in any international fixture is an achievement, but there were certainly signs, especially towards the end of the game, that we were becoming complacent. We were not always playing as sensibly as perhaps we should have been. The Italians were able to fight back and grab a couple of late scores. But 54–21 was a big one and very satisfying. The England selections were all justified but I don't think anyone was getting carried away. It was a positive start, and the right one for the team, but everyone knew that there were tougher times ahead, starting with New Zealand Barbarians one week later at Twickenham.

England 54 Italy 21

England	*Italy*
T Stimpson (Newcastle)	J Pertile (Roma)
J Sleightholme (Bath)	P Vaccari (Calvisano)
W Carling (Harlequins)	S Bordon (Rovigo)
P de Glanville (Bath)	I Francescato (Treviso)
A Adebayo (Bath)	L Manteri (Treviso)
M Catt (Bath)	D Dominguez (Milan)
A Gomarsall (Wasps)	A Troncon (Treviso)
G Rowntree (Leicester)	M Cuttitta (Milan)
M Regan (Bristol)	C Orlandi (Milan)
J Leonard (Harlequins)	F Properzi Curti (Milan)
T Rodber (Northampton)	M Giovanelli (PUC)
M Johnson (Leicester)	W Christofoletto (Treviso)
S Shaw (Bristol)	C Checchinato (Treviso)
L Dallaglio (Wasps)	C Covi (Padova)
C Sheasby (Wasps)	O Arancio (Milan)

Scorers
England. Tries: Gomarsall (2), Sleightholme, Dallaglio, Johnson, Rodber, Sheasby. Penalties: Catt (3). Conversions: Catt (5).
Italy. Tries: Vaccari, Troncon, Arancio. Conversions: Dominguez (3).

Replacements
England: J Leonard replaced by R Hardwick (Coventry; 71 minutes), M Regan replaced by P Greening (Gloucester; 77), A Gomarsall replaced by K Bracken (Saracens; 80).
Italy: C Covi replaced by A Sgorlon (Treviso; 58), C Checchinato replaced by A Barratin (Tarvisium; 80), A Troncon temporarily replaced by G Guidi (33–36 and 63–65).

30 NOVEMBER 1996

International match:
England 19 New Zealand Barbarians 34

It wasn't an official Test but it was undoubtedly a world class New Zealand team in opposition, even though the Kiwis said that it was only a Barbarians team. The All Blacks had just come off the back of what was probably their most successful season ever and had been rightly acclaimed as the best side in the world.

It was a huge challenge for us. New Zealand are the bench mark at the moment in world rugby and if there was an official ranking they would probably hold the top spot. The game gave us a chance to establish where England were in terms of world rugby, and what we could realistically hope to achieve over the next couple of years. I had never had any previous experience of fifteen-a-side rugby against any New Zealand outfit so it was a whole new experience for me. We had a number of players who went out on the Lions' tour, who had won and lost to them when the stakes had been high. That enabled us to get an idea of what we were going into. We needed to move forward and get meaningful fixtures and here we were playing New Zealand, probably the most meaningful of all. I think most of the squad were actually licking their lips at the prospect of pitting themselves against some of the best players in the world at Twickenham. You could not ask to play a better side, and for me to play against Michael Jones, whom I have always looked up to as one of the best players that has ever lived, was great.

People thought that New Zealand were going to win, but when people talk down your chances of winning it seems to bring out the best in everything that is English, that Bulldog spirit, that backs-against-the-wall attitude. People writing us off gave us added incentive and motivation. The intensity of the training that week was on a different level to that for the Italy game the week before. Perhaps that is a lesson we should learn – that if we can be that focused and that prepared then we can go on and do great things.

We were very confident that we could match them up front, that we had a scrum that was capable of taking them on. We were confident that we could win our own ball in the line-out, and disrupt theirs. The game was a chance for us to go out and achieve something big. We knew we would have a full house at Twickenham and everyone approached it as a full international. It did not have a Barbarian feel about it, it was as intense as any game that I have played in. It was England–New Zealand as far as we were concerned whether they were wearing red, white or blue.

The pace of the game was far quicker, the willingness to run the ball was far greater, the hits were much harder and the concentration level was higher than in any other game I had ever been involved in. For a number of the players involved it was an eye-opener, showing how Test rugby should be played. We performed well and were better than New Zealand at times. We put them under a lot of pressure – our tackling was the best it had been for a long time; we were knocking them down. There were moments in the game when the brilliance of Christian Cullen took them through our first line of defence and it took some desperate tackling to keep them out. But keep them out we did, and we then started to take the game to them. We created overlaps and scored a couple of tries. However, although we tackled superbly throughout the team, we did lose concentration a couple of times. The pressure put on us forced mistakes – we kicked badly, we box-kicked badly, we seemed to kick balls straight down their throats. When you give guys like Cullen and Jonah Lomu that kind of space and the opportunity to run back at you you're making a rod for your own back. But there were positive signs for us: some of the inter-passing between the forwards, the ball retention and the willingness to strike out wide. We competed in the scrum, we competed in the line-out and Simon Shaw had a massive game against Ian Jones. It was a good learning experience for everyone involved but while we competed for sixty minutes they taught us a lot of lessons and ran out comfortable winners.

England 19 New Zealand Barbarians 34

England	*New Zealand Barbarians*
T Stimpson (Newcastle)	C Cullen (Manawatu)
J Sleightholme (Bath)	J Vidiri (Counties)
W Carling (Harlequins)	A Ieremia (Wellington)
P de Glanville (Bath)	L Stensness (Auckland)
A Adebayo (Bath)	J Lomu (Counties)
M Catt (Bath)	A Mehrtens (Canterbury)
A Gomarsall (Wasps)	J Marshall (Canterbury)
G Rowntree (Leicester)	M Allen (Taranaki)
M Regan (Bristol)	S Fitzpatrick (Auckland)
J Leonard (Harlequins)	O Brown (Auckland)
T Rodber (Northampton)	M Jones (Auckland)
M Johnson (Leicester)	I Jones (North Harbour)
S Shaw (Bristol)	R Brooke (Auckland)
L Dallaglio (Wasps)	A Blowers (Auckland)
C Sheasby (Wasps)	T Randall (Otago)

Scorers
England. Tries: Sleightholme, Stimpson. Penalties: Catt (3).
New Zealand Barbarians. Tries: Brooke, Blowers, Spencer, Vidiri. Penalties: Mehrtens (2), Spencer (2). Conversion: Spencer.

Replacements
New Zealand Barbarians: T Randell replaced by D Mika (Auckland; 57 minutes), A Mehrtens replaced by C Spencer (Auckland; 60), J Vidiri replaced by G Osborne (North Harbour; 80).

The substitution issue is one that is very vivid in my mind because the pace of this game was relentless. There was no harm in replacing some very weary legs and I think they chose to do that at the first available opportunity which was fair enough. But when they felt that perhaps they were in danger of losing the game they made changes, and they brought on Carlos Spencer at fly half. This seemed to kick them up into another gear and they became so much more dynamic. I felt that we could have made substitutions but didn't because it is not in our nature. Professional rugby has only been here a few months and we have yet to learn that substitutions in a squad system is part of professional sport. If you take a player off it doesn't automatically mean a slur on his performance. Why not get some fresh legs on and some words of advice from the bench down to the side line? The New Zealand Barbarians made substitutions at a critical moment in the game and Carlos Spencer came on and made an immediate impact.

I was surprised that the Press didn't pick up on the substitution issue after the game. We had six quality players on the bench. Anyone can bring on substitutes when you are sixty or seventy points up, but the key to a good substitution is bringing the right one on at a crucial time in the game. It seemed as though New Zealand could up the tempo whenever they wanted and I think that that is a consequence of their players being comfortable with the idea of tactical substitution at that level of rugby. I have never yet been substituted in this manner but no doubt the time will come. You have to respect the person who makes that decision, they would not take you off unless they felt that the person coming on could do a better job.

It is clear that if we are going to move forward as a rugby playing nation we need to play the southern hemisphere teams on a much more regular basis. The level of intensity and pressure that the game brought was immense, but it was very refreshing to play in an open game where guys weren't killing the ball, where it was all about making big hits and big tackles and getting up and making another one. I am sure that lessons have been taken on board. Our players need to be exposed to that level of intensity and pressure if we are going to survive and have a realistic chance of winning the World Cup.

I had met Sean Fitzpatrick, the All Blacks' captain and hooker, a couple of months beforehand and realised then that the Kiwis, who have achieved everything, go on achieving because they go on wanting to improve. It is good to meet these guys because this attitude is so rare. They have been professional for a number of years now, regardless of what people say, and it shows.

4 Back On Track

7 DECEMBER 1996

Courage League Division One: Wasps 15 Bristol 12

To come out of a New Zealand game and have to go and play league rugby while trying to prepare for another international the following week seems to me to indicate that there are problems with the structure of the season, problems that need ironing out. After living together for a week with your England teammates, you have to go back to your club and train for a week, and then back to England again. It is like living out of a bag – you are in a hotel one week, then home for two or three days, then back to a hotel again. I am better off than some players because, playing for Wasps, I am at least London-based.

If we were to sustain a challenge in the league then Bristol was a must-win game. They had not been playing very well and we have a very proud record against them in the league, even though we have always had reasonably close games – there are no easy ones in the First Division. The league table had a very unusual look to it; Harlequins and Wasps were firmly one and two followed by Leicester and Bath. We went into this encounter under no illusions, but we did get a bit carried away.

We were winning comfortably but we weren't getting enough points on the board, and in the second half Bristol hit us with a huge shock, and suddenly the game seemed to be slipping away. They scored a converted try in the corner in the last five minutes of the game, taking a one-point lead. I then got everyone behind the posts and said, 'Look, believe we can win this; we have got one last attack and let's get up there to keep hold of the ball.' We managed to drive forward until there was a scrum on the left-hand corner of the pitch. We got ourselves together for one huge last effort, we had to throw everything at them. There were three collapsed scrums and then the referee gave a penalty, four minutes into injury time. John Ufton had had a miserable day, and it was a very difficult kick. As I picked the ball up, Alex King came up to me and said, 'I want to kick.' I don't know if he had had a word with John but I was relieved that his confidence had effectively taken the decision out of my hands. Alex is left footed so it was from the wrong side and he had not kicked under pressure all season. But he kicked it over and the referee immediately blew the final whistle and we had won. Bristol were gutted – they had deserved to win and we had been very fortunate.

Wasps 15 Bristol 13

Wasps	Bristol
J Ufton	P Hull
P Sampson	D Tiueti
N Greenstock	S Martin
V Tuigamala	M Denney
S Roiser	B Breeze
A King	P Burke
A Gomarsall	R Smith
D Molloy	A Sharp
S Mitchell	M Regan
W Green	D Hinkins
L Dallaglio	D Corkery
D Cronin	S Shaw
A Reed	C Eagle
M White	S Filali
C Sheasby	M Corry

Scorers
Wasps. Tries: King, White. Penalty: King. Conversion: Ufton.
Bristol: Tries: Hull, Corkery. Penalty: Burke.

Replacements
Wasps: W Green replaced by I Dunston (72 minutes).
Bristol: M Corry replaced by C Barrow (81).

14 DECEMBER 1996

International match: England 20 Argentina 18

Argentina had just been on tour and consequently had had a good build-up to the match at Twickenham. I think the public expectation was that Argentina should be rolled over fairly convincingly, as they were the last time they came over, especially as we were blessed with a lot of experience in the team – players who had already played against them at various levels. Argentina had employed the coaching services of New Zealander Grizz Wyllie, who had been the coach at Eastern Province when I played in South Africa in 1994. He was a very good, hard player and so it wasn't hard to guess how he was going to send his team out to play.

He had probably said something like, 'These English guys are soft, I've seen it all before. Let's get stuck into them, climb into them and get some boots on, that's the way to get through them.' The forwards were certainly going to be a very well drilled competitive outfit. It turned out to be quite a frustrating game, although not one that we ever thought we were going to lose. In the week leading up to the game we studied videos of South Africa's tour to Argentina, which included two Test matches. South Africa won both those games, but on the evidence of the video, they were made to work extremely hard for their victories. I don't think anyone was under any illusions about the threat that Argentina were able to pose. We knew from the World Cup that their set pieces were very strong, that they were one of the strongest scrummaging sides in the world and that they were competent in the line-out and even better in the loose. We realised that we were going to be in for a hard game.

It would have been nice to have fielded the same team that played against New Zealand, but that wasn't possible. Stimpson had concussion and Adebayo had got a nasty injury in a league game, and so those two were replaced by Tony Underwood and Nick Beale. I think no one was more surprised than Tony. I don't really think Tony felt that there would be much chance of getting selected after the disappointments of the last World Cup, and especially while playing lower league rugby for Newcastle. I was pleased for Nick Beale – I had played with him in the World Cup Sevens. He'd been a victim of his own versatility as a player. He never really settled down at Northampton in any one position because injuries to other players forced him to move about. This had probably cost him an earlier opportunity in international rugby but he was in good form and capable of doing a good job.

The training went reasonably well until the latter part of the week, coincidentally when we moved to the Petersham Hotel. Phil de Glanville sustained a dead leg during a fairly intense training session. Even as good a physio as Kevin Murphy could only do a certain amount. It was especially disappointing for Phil to miss leading the team out at Twickenham. I know, from being a club captain, that if your team's just lost a match, as we just had against the New Zealand Barbarians, it's important that you bounce back very quickly and repair the damage. The Argentina game was the ideal opportunity for us to do that. What's more, it was a home game so we would have a big crowd on our side.

As Phil was captain he was given until Saturday to announce his fitness when, quite sensibly, he said it was not going to work. This gave the public what they wanted to see – an in-form Guscott playing alongside an in-form Carling. The ingredients were there to really sign off the year in style. It did mean a change of captaincy and Jason Leonard took over. Even before Phil was appointed captain, Jason would take the scrummaging sessions and quite rightly so: he's the most experienced forward in the pack; he's been around a long time; technically he's far superior to any other prop; and he has the respect of the entire team. So he assumed the mantle of pack leader and with that I would imagine the mantle of vice-captain. I don't think Jack had any problem in making him captain for that particular match.

The message from within was that we had played one game against Italy, we had played the New Zealand game, and what we needed to do now was to incorporate everything that went well in both those two games and really try and put together a decent performance for a full eighty minutes. It didn't work out like that at all and we felt that we had let ourselves down. It's no excuse, but for me the ball seemed to be out of play the whole time. We didn't seem to get our hands on the ball and even when we did we made mistakes. There were a lot of penalties on both sides. We just never seemed to get going really and it became very frustrating. We had a Guscott try disallowed because Martin Johnson was penalised for an infringement. We also had what I thought was a legitimate try disallowed right at the beginning. We drove one over, and had we scored then perhaps that would have calmed the nerves down a little bit. Perhaps Argentina should be given credit, they came to play and to defend. They were determined not to suffer the same humiliation that they suffered at Twickenham in 1990 when they lost 51–0. I've always said that the sign of a good team is one that can play badly and still win matches. At international level it is exactly the same thing. We were playing badly, we accept that but we had to dog it out and win. We were losing, the crowd were getting uneasy, and the game was drawing to the finish.

In the last quarter, we got a penalty, and ironically scored a very similar try to the one South Africa scored against Argentina. I was very pleased for Jason Leonard that he scored a try when captaining the side. Props don't get many tries but he scored one of the most important tries of the season. There was genuine disappointment afterwards, not just because we played badly but because we had been together now for three weeks as a squad, getting a feel of each other's abilities. Individually and collectively we can play much better. There certainly wasn't a sense of panic, everyone accepted the fact that we played badly, that certain bad decisions were made. We'd done what it took to win the game in the circumstances. I think it made a lot of people anxious about selection, which is not what you want when you are going into the Five Nations'. On the other hand, perhaps it was important that people needed to be told that they have got to perform to a certain standard every time for England or others will come and take your place. The euphoria that had brought in the five new caps at the beginning of the season had now settled down. Argentina had exposed certain weaknesses in the team which you wouldn't want to see again. But in the longer term it's better that they were exposed now rather than in the semi-final of the World Cup against New Zealand.

England 20 Argentina 18

England	*Argentina*
N Beal (Northampton)	E Jurado (Jockey Rosario)
J Sleightholme (Bath)	G Camardon (Alumni)
W Carling (Harlequins)	E Simone (Liceo Naval)
J Guscott (Bath)	L Arbizu (Belgrano)
T Underwood (Newcastle)	D Albanese (SIC)
M Catt (Bath)	G Quesada (Hindu)
A Gomarsall (Wasps)	N Fernandez Miranda (Hindu)
G Rowntree (Leicester)	R Grau (Licea)
M Regan (Bristol)	C Promanzio (Duendes)
J Leonard (Harlequins)	M Reggiardo (Castres)
T Rodber (Northampton)	R Martin (SIC)
M Johnson (Leicester)	P Sporleder (Curupayti)
S Shaw (Bristol)	G Llanes (La Plata)
L Dallaglio (Wasps)	P Camerlinckx (Ragatas Bella Vista)
C Sheasby (Wasps)	P Bouza (Duendes)

Scorers
England. Try: Leonard. Penalties: Catt (5).
Argentina. Penalties: Queseda (6).

Replacements
England: C Sheasby replaced by B Clarke (Richmond; 56 minutes).

21 DECEMBER 1996

Pilkington Cup Round 5: Wasps 84 Rugby Lions 8

After the Argentina game the draw was made for the fifth round of the Pilkington Cup and it provided, from our point of view, a welcome relief on two fronts. We got a home fixture, which is rare for Wasps in this competition and we drew Rugby Lions, which gave us a chance to re-focus and get our shape back. They had just lost 150–0 to Newcastle so we weren't too worried by the threat they might pose. The Pilkington Cup is never going to be like the FA Cup, with the dream of the smaller team becoming successful. It used to work occasionally in rugby, but to bridge the gap between the two divisions in the new professional age would be tremendously difficult. The gulf between bottom and top of the division has become wider, and therefore it creates a bit of a mismatch. It has now become difficult to market this sort of game because the results are almost a foregone conclusion – it's just a question of how many points are the top teams going to score. However, it was nice to play at Sudbury again. The game itself was like a throwback, a reminder of the past when Rugby were First Division material and we used to play each other on a regular basis, but the fact that we ran in fourteen tries to win 84–8 was an indication that the gap will continue to grow.

We realised that there were some very important league games coming up and there was no doubt that the pre-Christmas international programme had had a damaging effect, not just on Wasps but on every club. Players lose their focus after experiencing the emotional highs of international games but it is essential that they can put all that to one side when they return to the club environment. It is worth remembering that it is a player's performance at club level which takes him into the national arena. Fortunately, it's not so bad for Wasps because we don't have as many England internationals as some clubs.

I am a fan of Chelsea FC and know they used to play on Christmas Eve, Boxing Day and New Year's Day but I never expected to see that sort of scheduling in rugby. However, now we had a pretty hectic Christmas schedule ourselves, training nearly every day apart from Christmas Day. We felt that if we could start well after Christmas, still at the top of the league, then we would be in with a shout in the home straight. That was the message we were hammering into the players. That next batch of league games was going to be so important.

Christmas is always a very difficult time for our family, principally because my sister Francesca, who died in the 1989 Marchioness boat disaster, had her birthday on 29 December. It brings back quite emotive memories for my parents and so we now go away on holiday at Christmas. My parents used to go away and I would spend Christmas with some friends. They would either go down to some relations in England or fly to somewhere sunny. We had always been such a close-knit family at Christmas, so it's very difficult to try and re-create that when one member of the family is not there. Time is a great healer and as the years have gone by it's become easier. But this year was a bit different: I was with Alice and we were expecting our first child. I'd told my mother about a month previously and she was absolutely delighted; the fact that she was going to have a grandchild aided the healing process. She was already saying it was going to be a daughter. Alice and I went to my parents for Christmas Day and had a really nice time, although I didn't tuck into too much of the food because I was training the next morning. It was my first sober Christmas for a number of years. It was quite a strange feeling. We didn't crack open the bottle of vintage port as we normally do, but I enjoyed the food more than ever before – because I could actually taste it.

28 DECEMBER 1996

Courage League Divsion One: Wasps 18 Northampton 13

We were training for the Northampton game and looking forward to it as much as ever. It was a game we had to win and we knew that they posed quite a threat. Their scrum half, Matt Dawson, was injured, which was a plus for us but disappointing for Andy Gomarsall who was dying to have a snap at his heels. Dawson had lost his place in the England squad to Gomarsall and so he was desperate to play in this sort of game. Despite his absence Northampton still had a very strong side with Paul Grayson and Gregor Townsend in the backs. They had both played fly half at international level, Paul for England and Gregor for Scotland. Gregor was now playing at centre for Northampton and he looked about as comfortable there as I had been playing open side. I couldn't see much future for him in that role. Gregor should have been playing at stand off – it would have suited Northampton's style of rugby.

They played superbly, it was the first time in the whole season that we hadn't scored a try in a league game, and if it hadn't have been for Gareth Rees, we wouldn't have won the match. His goal kicking was exemplary – he kicked six out of six. I think Northampton had the greater share of possession but didn't do the right thing with it. Paul Grayson was off with his boot, which is not something you see too often. He missed a couple of early kicks which would have put us under a lot of pressure. Northampton are very good at recycling ball; they're a very fit side, they can certainly run around and play for eighty-five minutes without any problem. Mind you, they need to because they do like to throw the ball. They throw the ball wide from the first phase and ask the people out wide to do something with it. There's nothing wrong with that provided the people out wide get you over the gain line – it's an option favoured by New Zealand. When you pass the ball out wide you're passing the responsibility as well, and we found it very easy to defend because they didn't create the necessary overlaps. They played man on man, and so didn't draw in enough defenders in order to throw it wide.

What we did very well in that game was to only commit one, or at the maximum two men, to the tackle. They would spin it wide and we would have enough cover to get there. Perhaps if they'd taken it through the middle of our pack we would have been drawn in or taken around the fringes, and they would have scored out wide, but we managed to keep them out for large periods of the game. They scored one try in the first half but, as much as they applied the pressure we stayed calm and made our tackles. When we did have the ball we took it onto them and they infringed. I'm a firm believer that if sides are going to infringe then they should be punished, and they should realise that every time they give a penalty away against us, it's going to be three points because there's no one better in the English game at punishing infringements than Gareth Rees.

Wasps 18 Northampton 13

Wasps	Northampton
G Rees	N Beal
S Roiser	I Hunter
N Greenstock	M Allen
A James	R MacNaughton
V Tuigamala	H Thorneycroft
A King	P Grayson
A Gomarsall	D Malone
M Griffiths	M Volland
S Mitchell	A Clarke
W Green	G Walsh
L Dallaglio	S Tatupu
D Cronin	J Phillips
A Reed	J Chandler
M White	A Pountney
C Sheasby	T Rodber

Scorers
Wasps. Penalties: Rees (6).
Northampton. Try: Chandler. Penalties: Grayson (2). Conversions:
Grayson (2).

Replacements
Wasps: M Griffiths replaced by D Molloy (57 minutes), D Cronin
replaced by R Kinsey (57), S Mitchell replaced by D Macer (80).
Northampton: T Rodber replaced by J Cassell (80).

5 Out of the Cup

For New Year, Andy Gomarsall organised a dinner party at his house in Oxford and I went along with Alice, who was by then heavily pregnant – only three months to go. We had a nice quiet night. There were about twenty of us in all and everyone else went out to a nightclub just before midnight, which left Alice and I indoors with a bottle of champagne celebrating a rather romantic New Year's Eve. It was good fun, and it was probably the first New Year's Day for a long time where I hadn't woken up with a raging hangover – strange, but definitely good.

The start of the New Year wasn't all good as, that same day, I was stopped for speeding while driving back to London on a deserted M40. I had only just got my licence back in the October after serving a six-month ban. One of my New Year's resolutions had been to stop speeding so it was disappointing, especially as my BMW doesn't seem comfortable at anything less than 80 mph. I don't know, now that Dean Richards has retired the police seem to book everyone!

4 JANUARY 1997

Courage League Division One: Wasps 17 Harlequins 19

Having won seven games on the trot, I think I was quite justified in going into this game in confident mood. The media were trying to build it up as *the* London derby and I fell for the sucker punch which probably gave Harlequins just the sort of motivation they needed to get themselves up for the match. I did an interview with Mike Wedderburn for *Rugby Special*. He played for Harlequins and for Wasps, and he was doing an interview after the Northampton game. He said, 'Are you looking forward to the London derby – Harlequins v. Wasps?' I said that I was, and then added something like 'the Kings of London against the Harlequeens.' I understand Dick Best played this over and over again in his motivational team talks. I don't think any of my teammates would thank me for saying it because it really fired them up and got them going for the game. But I felt it was the type of hype that's missing in rugby sometimes. I think that little things like that don't do the sport any harm. Perhaps it should come from someone who sits fairly evenly in the middle though. I didn't mean too much by it, but obviously they took it very seriously.

It was another Sunday fixture at Loftus Road and we hadn't yet lost in the league there, so trying to make the home ground an impregnable fortress was still a very realistic ambition. We'd beaten some good sides there, so it was important we kept the momentum going. I wasn't surprised by the Harlequins team selection. Gary Connolly, a very talented player, was playing in the centre – he had become a huge success after switching from Rugby League, both on and off the pitch.

The game started in typical derby fashion, at one hundred miles an hour. For the first twenty-five minutes we played very well, a lot better than we had been playing in the last few league games. Gareth had a few penalties, but he wasn't as accurate as he had been of late and so was unable to settle our nerves. Then we got a try in the left-hand corner and we had the game by the scruff of the neck. It was looking as though it was going to be close, but that we would win. Then we let them right back in the game. Quins had absorbed our pressure quite well and then came back at us, playing a territorial game. Thierry Lacroix knocked over any penalty we gave them. He showed the value that they put on him with an immaculate kicking display, and against the team that Harlequins most wanted to beat. In the second half the one tackle we missed in the backs cost us a try when Connolly went in under the posts. It was a game we felt we could have won, but Quins took their chances very well.

We had ridden our luck in the last couple of games and this was one of those games where the luck wasn't with us and we lost by the narrowest of margins. At Wasps we've always prided ourselves on the fact that when we lose a game we take it very personally – each individual takes a long, hard look at their own performance. And what Wasps have been very good at is responding to defeats. Earlier on in the season, in Europe, we had to lose a couple of games before the guys started pulling themselves round again. But this time, although we were very disappointed that we'd lost our home record against Harlequins, we were determined to pick things up again.

Wasps 17 Harlequins 19

Wasps	Harlequins
G Rees	R Paul
J Ufton	D Luger
N Greenstock	G Connolly
V Tuigamala	W Carling
S Roiser	P Mensah
A King	T Lacroix
A Gomarsall	H Harries
D Molloy	L Benezech
S Mitchell	P Delaney
W Green	J Leonard
L Dallaglio	R Jenkins
A Reed	Glyn Llewellyn
D Cronin	Gareth Llewellyn
M White	L Cabannes
C Sheasby	W Davison

Scorers
Wasps. Try: Cronin. Penalties: Rees (3). Dropped goal: King.
Harlequins. Try: Connolly. Penalties: Lacroix (4). Conversion: Lacroix.

Replacements
Wasps: D Cronin replaced by R Kinsey (78 minutes), M White replaced by I Dunston (78).
Harlequins: P Mensah replaced by C Wright (17), R Jenkins replaced by M Watson (79).

11 JANUARY 1997

Courage League Division One: Bristol 18 Wasps 41

At this time we were under the impression that Inga Tuigamala was to go back to Wigan. There were discussions going on between Chris Wright, Nigel Melville, Wigan and Inga's agent with regard to him staying on at Wasps with us buying him out of his contract. His influence on the club and on the team had been huge and the possibility that the match at Bristol might be his last game for Wasps focused everyone's minds on really sending him off with a performance to remember.

It always seems to be very dark and overcast at Bristol, and this day was no exception. The game was an important test for us and it was important that the message be sent out to everyone that the Harlequins game had just been a little blip. The nice thing about this season was that if you lost one game it wasn't the end of the world. Other sides were losing games around us as well. But we knew this was a crunch game and, before a full house at Bristol, we certainly didn't have it all our own way. We played with quite a bit of authority but then Bristol came back at us. They certainly had chances to score but our defence was superb and we held firm. Shortly before half time they had a move which broke down right on our goal line. We ended up running it back the length of the field for Shane Roiser to score. That gave us a bit of breathing space and then in the second half we played a very controlled game before cutting loose at the end when Inga scored two tries to mark his last game for us. The second try was a run around and he was happy to have the opportunity to sign off in style. We scored six tries in all and ran out comfortable winners. We were quite pleased with the result – it gave us a platform to build on as we entered the second and hardest part of the season.

Bristol 18 Wasps 41

Bristol	*Wasps*
P Hull	G Rees
D Tiueti	J Ufton
S Martin	N Greenstock
M Denney	V Tuigamala
B Breeze	S Roiser
P Burke	A King
R Jones	A Gomarsall
A Sharp	D Molloy
M Regan	D Macer
D Hinkins	W Green
M Corry	L Dallaglio
P Adams	D Cronin
C Eagle	A Reed
D Corkery	C Sheasby
E Rollitt	M White

Scorers
Bristol. Tries: Denney, Burke. Penalties: Burke (2). Conversion: Burke.
Wasps. Tries: Tuigamala (2), Reed, Greenstock, Roiser, Sheasby. Penalty: Rees. Conversions: Rees (4).

Replacements
Bristol: M Denney replaced by K Maggs (50 minutes).
Wasps: D Cronin replaced by R Kinsey (72), W Green replaced by I Dunston (75), A Gomarsall replaced by J Wood (77), D Macer replaced by K Dunn (78).

On the way back from Bristol there were only ten or twelve of us on the bus enjoying a few beers after the game. We were about half way through the journey, when the coach suddenly braked and I went flying into the toilet and hit my head. There had been a crash right in front of us, on the middle lane of the motorway – a Land Rover had spun out of control, gone through the central reservation and hit a ditch. All the lads ran out to see what was going on. The vehicle was on its roof, the wheels were still spinning, the two drivers were trapped inside and there was diesel and glass everywhere. It is quite unsettling to arrive seconds after a crash, not really knowing what to do, fearing for the driver and wondering if the car is about to blow up. The situation was certainly dangerous but they couldn't have had anyone better around: we had a medical team on board, a doctor and a physio, and we had a lot of the pack on board, so the stronger players were able to rip one door off and drag the two guys out. They were bleeding and concussed and didn't really know what was going on. Fortunately, our manager, Malcolm Sinclair, is an ex-policeman so he was able to direct the traffic away from danger. It was uncanny: we had the police force, the medical team, and the heavies to do the lifting.

It was a lucky escape for the two lads who later wrote to the club. They had been out on a shooting trip. They had never really followed rugby, but they swore they would support Wasps for the rest of their lives. One was a publican who promised to share a barrel of beer with us, so it was a happy ending for all concerned. It was also quite interesting that the first policeman on the scene was the same policeman who had stopped me for speeding on New Year's Day. We recognised one another even though I had six stitches in my eye and blood and diesel all over me when he turned up. We had a laugh and joke about the different circumstances under which we had met.

The next event at the club was the Quinquennial dinner, a chance for everyone to catch up. There were tables for all the big-name players who played in the 1930s, 1940s, 1950s, 1960s, 1970s and 1980s, so each generation was well represented. It was a chance for people who have played the game to share conversation with the players who are currently playing the game and vice versa. It was a nice chance to meet old and new faces in the club and it is always a good evening, the players love going there. This year was a little bit difficult for me as I was away in a hotel in Marlow preparing for the England–France game. This was my first Quinquennial dinner, and, as captain of the club, I had been called upon to make a speech. In the end it didn't prove too difficult, although I am not the greatest after dinner speaker. But when you are talking amongst the Wasps you are talking amongst your family, you can just speak from the heart. However, I have to admit to being a little nervous beforehand, but with the England game coming up I could not have a relaxing drink.

I sat on the top table, between Wasps' president Bill Treadwell and the president of the RFU, John Richardson. Jack Rowell sat opposite. Alice was also there, and that made me even more nervous. I felt it was my duty to speak about what had happened over the last five years and I also paid tribute to a lot of people who perhaps would have otherwise gone unmentioned. I wanted to reflect on the way things were going, what the future held for Wasps and generally talk about the game, while trying to be funny at the same time. The speechmakers also included John Richardson, Bill Treadwell, David Trick, Mark Bailey and finally Willie John McBride. It was a good night.

The only upsetting thing for me was that I had to dash off so quickly after dinner. I left at about midnight, straight after the speeches, when there were still so many faces from the past that I hadn't had a chance to speak to, people like the former back row man Frances Emeruwa. I hadn't seen him at the club for two or three years and it would have been good to have spent some time with him. I remembered that the last time that I was at the Savoy Hotel I was working as a luggage porter for the concierge desk, and now I was speaking in front of 700 people at the Quinquennial dinner. It was quite amusing because I have seen what happens behind the scenes – my father has been in catering all his life and he still works at the Savoy Hotel as a consultant so it was nice to see how the other half live.

22 January 1997

Anglo-Welsh Cup: Wasps v. Bridgend. Cancelled.

When this game was cancelled everyone realised the Anglo-Welsh competition was going down the tubes. If it was to continue, we would use it for extended training, and as a chance to develop players and bring them on. We had spent a lot of money getting down there to play the first game and the compliment wasn't being returned, so it was a bit of a disappointment.

25 JANUARY 1997

Pilkington Cup Round 6: Saracens 21 Wasps 17

If we were to get to the final of the Pilkington Cup then we had to beat anyone and everyone in our way, but this was never going to be an easy fixture. They were unbeaten at their Enfield home, so it was going to be extremely difficult. We knew the areas where we could win the game and knew that their main threat would come from Michael Lynagh at stand off, not just because of his goal kicking but also through his tactical appreciation of the game, his field play and his line kicking. He also had a point to prove – he'd gone off with a dislocated shoulder in our first meeting. He certainly didn't let anyone down on the day. We'd really overwhelmed them up front at Loftus Road, and so I'm sure they felt that they needed to get a little bit more physical, a little bit tougher and their world class South African flanker Francois Pienaar was certainly capable of bringing a little bit of that into the equation. He has his critics but he is a very strong rugby player and very aggressive in his loose play. It was clear that the Saracens team had been galvanised into really being up for the game.

When we went to Enfield we found quite poor facilities for a visiting team. The facilities that we've provided for teams in the past have not been the best but in a new professional age we realised that they needed to be improved. That was one of the reasons we moved to Loftus Road where both sides get the same treatment. But when we turned up at Saracens we were given a Portacabin to change in. To fit fifteen players and a back-up team comprising six substitutes, coaching staff, medical staff, equipment and so on into a Portacabin was difficult, to say the least. To be expected to do so was appalling. I felt that it showed a lack of respect. It created an environment in which it was very difficult to prepare. It felt as though you were changing in an old shed before going out to play a benefit game for someone. The environment didn't befit a team of high status, and it made it hard for us to get a focus for the match.

We went out to play and were immediately hit by a very determined Saracens team who were obviously disappointed at the way they had played at Loftus Road. They were short of ambition and played a game that relied on kicking the lines. They didn't score a try against us but Lynagh scored twenty-one points, through two dropped goals and five penalties. For the first time in a long while we were muscled out of the game up front, but we allowed it to happen. We were beaten to first phase, we were invariably turned over in tackles, we were pushed off the ball and we were wheeled sufficiently to give their back row an advantage. The calmness and the coolness under pressure which we had displayed in a lot of the bigger games was abandoned, they took advantage, played exceptionally well and ran out worthy winners.

There aren't many teams that have outplayed us and we knew that the reason we lost the game was because we had let ourselves down. We didn't play well enough to win the game. We didn't deserve to win, and now we were out of the Pilkington Cup as well as being out of Europe. The only positive thing to come out of it was that we could now concentrate solely on the league as we now had nothing else to distract us. We were the first of the more fancied teams in the league which could say that, although Bath followed shortly afterwards when they were knocked out by Leicester.

I left Saracens pretty much straight away. I am a bad loser, but I usually give the opposition the respect they deserve and go and have a drink with them and say well done. I was already thinking about the following week's game and how we would put things right. I really just needed to go home and be on my own. I was extremely disappointed, not only with my own performance but also with my teammates'. The only thing that brightened me up slightly was trying to find signs for somewhere, anywhere that I vaguely recognised as being in the direction of home. I turned on Radio 5 Live and listened to commentary on the FA Cup quarter final between Chelsea and Liverpool. It was 2–2 at the time and the commentator was reeling off superlatives about what a wonderful game it was. I managed to get back home in time to watch the last fifteen minutes and see Chelsea score again and win the match. That cheered me up slightly but I was still disappointed at losing to Saracens. Saracens aren't supposed to beat Wasps; Wasps are supposed to be one of the strongest teams in London, if not the strongest. It went against the norm and it annoyed me intensely.

Saracens 21 Wasps 17

Saracens	*Wasps*
M Evans	G Rees
K Chesney	J Ufton
P Sella	A James
S Ravenscroft	N Greenstock
R Wallace	S Roiser
M Lynagh	G Gregory
K Bracken	A Gomarsall
A Daly	D Molloy
G Botterman	D Macer
P Wallace	W Green
F Pienaar	L Dallaglio
P Johns	D Cronin

A Copsey	R Kinsey
R Hill	M White
A Diprose	C Sheasby

Scorers
Saracens. Penalties: Lynagh (5). Dropped goals: Lynagh (2).
Wasps. Try: White. Penalties: Rees (4).

Replacements
Wasps: D Macer replaced by S Mitchell (62 minutes), J Ufton replaced by M Wood (82).

6 The Five Nations' Championship

1 FEBRUARY 1997

Five Nations' Championship: England 41 Scotland 13

The Five Nations' squad had been announced at the beginning of the week, before the Pilkington Cup match. I'd been quite nervous about selection for a number of reasons. We hadn't played well collectively against Argentina and there was some controversy about which was my best position. I had played open side for all of my seven England appearances yet I was playing blind side for Wasps. Although people were saying that I was doing very well, even that I was the new Peter Winterbottom I knew there would be tougher times ahead if I was going to continue playing my international rugby in that position. Sooner or later the pressure would start coming from Jack Rowell and others who would want to know why I was playing blind side for my club when that wasn't helping England at all. It was becoming increasingly difficult from Jack's point of view to justify picking me at open side when week in, week out I was playing blind side for Wasps.

My last match for England had been against Argentina at open side and I had had a very quiet game. I was very worried about making the team. Jack phoned me up just after the New Year – and made his point concerning the different positions. When Jack first asked me to play open side, I wanted to play for England so much that I said that I would be happy playing there and that I wanted to do it.

I knew that at some point I would have to tell him that what I really wanted was to play on the blind side. If that meant being dropped for a year or two, I would have to bite the bullet, because in the long term that would be a better option for my own happiness. The question of when to tell Jack was becoming increasingly urgent and I just felt that this conversation was the time to do it. We had a chat about Wasps, about England and the three pre-Christmas internationals and how we felt they went. Then I told him that I felt my strengths as a rugby player were running at people, ball in hand, and taking people on – something I could do more easily at blind side, the position where I felt most comfortable. I said that I thought that I was the best blind side in the country at the time. I had to say it, I had to get it off my chest. Jack took it all on board, but didn't give me any clues as to what he was thinking. He didn't give anything away. I thought that if I was dropped I would fight my way back and make sure I was picked at blind side.

Another factor making me worry about my place was that everyone in the Press was talking about the balance of the back row (Ben Clarke, Tim Rodber and myself) and saying that it wasn't right. The front five had shown that they were capable of competing with anyone in the world and what we needed now was to get the balance in the back row right. When the team was announced with me at blind side it was almost like getting picked for the first time all over again. The feeling of elation was very similar to the one I'd had when I got my first cap. Finally, I was going to be able to go out on the pitch and do myself justice, and not be wandering around with a map and a compass.

Tim Stimpson was restored at full back. He had done exceptionally well, particularly in the New Zealand game where he had made a couple of outstanding tackles on Lomu and had been very solid under the high ball, but we had yet to realise his attacking potential. He scored a nice try against New Zealand, when we eventually got the ball wide but we felt that we were yet to exploit him fully in the wider channels. However, if there was a full back who could break the line and come in strongly it was him. The right wing was Jon Sleightholme. Some people are quite critical about him, but he has got pace and a nose for the try line and is a great finisher. He scored tries against Italy and New Zealand, and given any ball against Argentina he'd probably have done the same to them. Will Carling was playing magnificent club rugby and Phil de Glanville was fit again so it was a pretty straightforward decision at centre, although it raised a few eyebrows that Jerry Guscott wasn't going to start the Five Nations' when he was in superlative form for Bath.

Paul Grayson came back at fly half. I might be biased, but I felt that we could have experimented and picked Wasps' fly half Alex King for the Argentina game. I don't think it would have done any harm at all. I think we could have picked King and then, if he hadn't done well we could have gone for Paul Grayson for the Five Nations'. But Paul came in and played very, very well – I think he certainly has the temperament for international rugby. He proved that last season, kicking goals at Twickenham when the crowd were booing him. People were quite critical about his game and saying that he played too deep and only kicked, but now he's got a much better all round game. The management knew that Paul would be solid, that they wouldn't be biting their nails in the stands. It was a risk though, there's no doubt about that. Andy Gomarsall was relieved to get selected for his first Five Nations' game – there was a lot of competition at scrum half. The two scrum halves from last season, Bracken and Dawson, were both out of the squad and Austin Healey was coming up very fast on the rails.

I was surprised that Richard Hill was picked at No. 7 because he lacked experience in the A team. I'd played with him in the back row in Australia in 1993 for England Under 21s. He was No. 8 and Tony Diprose was blind side. I was lucky enough to be the first out of the trio to get capped, but I always felt that the other two would not be far behind. Richard had certainly come right up to the front and had been the outstanding player of the domestic season. I believe it's only a matter of time before Tony Diprose joins the frame. Given Richard's lack of experience I felt the selectors might have gone for Neil Back who was making an extremely impressive claim for re-selection. It was clear that the choice was between the two of them and I was pleasantly surprised when they picked Richard Hill. Mind you I could picture Neil banging the door down and saying something like, 'Why are you picking Lawrence when he wants to play on the blind side? Why are you picking Ben Clarke when he's a No. 8? Why are you picking Steve Ojomoh when he's not a No. 7?' Richard was a bold selection, but at least everyone thought that we had actually picked someone who genuinely wanted to play open side, someone who played there week in, week out and did a very good job. We all agreed that he was good enough to do it for England.

Richard's worked very hard and I'm sure he believed it was only going to be a matter of time before he got capped. He's got a lot of belief in his own ability and the first couple of tackles he made in the Scotland game said it all really. He needs no encouragement from his teammates to get stuck in. I felt very confident going into the game with him because he's a fighter and he's going to give everything, whether you are going forwards or backwards.

The Five Nations' kicked off without England this year. There were two games before we even entered the competition, so we were able to sit back and watch. We could see how teams were approaching the international season, see who were going to be the danger men and we could work out what was going to be required to win the tournament. I watched Scotland v. Wales and France v. Ireland and saw the gauntlets being thrown down. We felt we had a powerful squad and that there were weaknesses in the Scottish team that we could exploit. There was definitely a feel-good factor about English rugby. Everyone at club level was much fitter and stronger, more mentally aware of what was going on around them and much more focused

Winning a line-out against Northampton

Top left Running out at Loftus
Road for the first time

Bottom left Perhaps our best
performance this season –
Wasps 77 Toulouse 17

Right In action against
Saracens . . .

Below . . . and Bath

Taking a breather against the New Zealand Barbarians

Recycling the ball against France

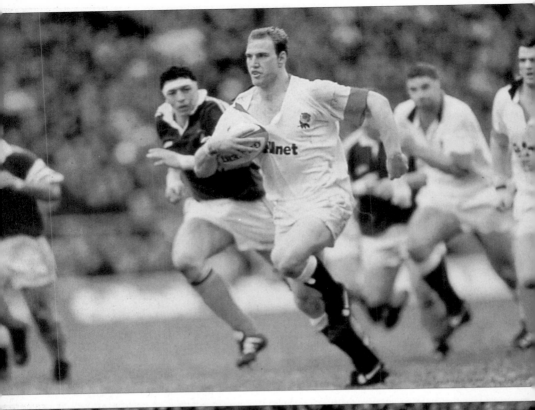

Top left On my way to the try line against France

Bottom left There's no way I'm going to let Phillippe Carbonneau stop me scoring

Right Acknowledging the Wasps fans – a great help to us all season

Below Celebrating with teammates after winning the league title

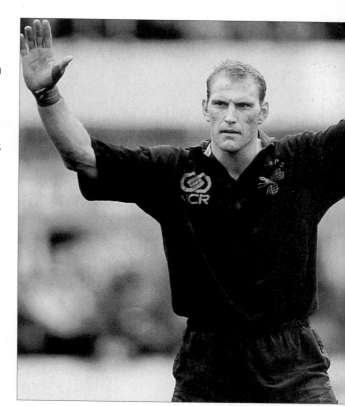

On the burst against Scotland

about each individual rugby match than ever before. But you're only as good as your last game, and our last game was not particularly good. So it was important that we got off to a flying start.

Scotland started with a lot of possession and Gregor Townsend was pretty clear about the way he wanted to play the game – he was running it from everywhere. Richard Hill caught him a couple of times with big hits to make his mark on the game. We felt comfortable, it was a good feeling to be back in the international arena, but Scotland got the first try, via Ronnie Ericksson after a missed tackle. Kenny Logan, who is now a good club pal of mine, managed to spin out of three or four tackles and fed the ball inside. All of a sudden, Scotland did pose a threat – they could score and they were 10–0 up. We had got a couple of penalties back when they had a line-out on our line. They threw it to Andy Reed at the front and drove us over; they were a couple of inches away from extending their lead. It would have been an uphill battle to have pulled back a twenty-point deficit. That kickstarted us into action and from then on we never looked back. The match was refereed in a very positive manner by Paddy O'Brien of New Zealand, who followed the philosophy of the southern hemisphere, tending to favour the attacking team. He gave the penalty try for persistent infringement – perhaps a little bit harsh in that we were still quite wide out, but I think he wanted to lay down his authority.

I felt that we were fitter than the Scots, but we needed a couple of tries to get the confidence back again. Eventually Martin Johnson broke free and fed Gomarsall who ran on to score – suddenly the shackles were off and we cut loose. This was our first Five Nations' game of the season and it was a record victory against Scotland. We had scored forty-one points and we were clearly off to a flying start. There were signs in that performance that England had the makings of a very good side indeed. If we could cut out the mistakes, we would be a very difficult side to beat in the championship.

The other significant development that day was the

resolution of the dispute between EPRUC and the RFU which had been going on since the end of the last season. It had been an on-going battle and had become so complicated that I think people gave up reading about it. On the day of the Scotland game announcements were made which indicated that we were now going to move forward on a united front. We were told that the nuts and bolts of the financial deals were still to be finalised, but that, in principle, the overriding issues had been resolved. The players found it surprising that nothing had been resolved before and felt that we should have already been enjoying the fruits of the professional era. We felt that we had to keep playing in order to ensure that, when the argument was finally resolved, there was still a game left on the pitch to fight over. And, of course, there was.

England 41 Scotland 13

England	*Scotland*
T Stimpson (Newcastle)	R Shepherd (Melrose)
J Sleightholme (Bath)	D Stark (Melrose)
W Carling (Harlequins)	A Stanger (Hawick)
P de Glanville (Bath)	B Eriksson (London Scottish)
T Underwood (Newcastle)	K Logan (Stirling County)
P Grayson (Northampton)	G Townsend (Northampton)
A Gomarsall (Wasps)	B Redpath (Melrose)
G Rowntree (Leicester)	T Smith (Watsonians)
M Regan (Bristol)	D Ellis (Currie)
J Leonard (Harlequins)	M Stewart (Northampton)
L Dallaglio (Wasps)	P Walton (Newcastle)
M Johnson (Leicester)	G Weir (Newcastle)
S Shaw (Bristol)	A Reed (Wasps)
R Hill (Saracens)	I Smith (Gloucester)
T Rodber (Northampton)	R Wainwright (Watsonians)

Scorers
England. Tries: Gomarsall, Carling, de Glanville, penalty try. Penalties: Grayson (5). Conversions: Grayson (3).
Scotland. Try: Eriksson. Penalties: Shepherd (2). Conversion: Shepherd.

Replacements
Scotland: B Eriksson replaced by S Hastings (Watsonians; 72 minutes).

8 FEBRUARY 1997

Courage League Division One: West Hartlepool 23 Wasps 48

There are no easy games in the First Division but this one did give us a chance to regain the confidence we had lost in the game against Saracens. We had to ask some players some harsh questions: What did they want to achieve this season? Did they want to finish off with having achieved nothing or did they want to ensure that the club won something, qualified for Europe and finished the season on a high? West Hartlepool has always been a popular trip because of the friendliness of the people there and the homeliness of the ground.

We went up the night before on the train. There were the usual things happening, except people were now using money instead of matches in the card schools – an indication of our new-found professional status, no doubt. We went into the game very confidently, despite the very windy conditions, and got off to a flying start, putting a lot of points on the board. We were almost out of sight by half time. We had a couple of lapses of concentration after the break and let them in for three soft tries at the end which really annoyed me. We scored seven tries but we let them in for three, which they didn't deserve. At the back of everyone's mind was the points difference. We knew that all we could do was keep winning, but if we could score a lot of points at the same time then that would put us in a stronger position.

One player whom I thought shone for them was Liam Botham; I am sure he has a promising future. We had Mickey Skinner for company on the way home. He had been up there doing a feature for a newspaper – an interview with Liam Botham no less. He came back with the Wasps and immediately started complaining about how we were all wearing too much hair gel and how times have changed.

West Hartlepool 23 Wasps 48

West Hartlepool	*Wasps*
M Silva	G Rees
M Wood	P Sampson
L Botham	N Greenstock
J Connolly	R Henderson
S John	S Roiser
C John	A King
P Harvey	A Gomarsall
J Painter	D Molloy
A Peacock	S Mitchell
W de Jonge	W Green
C Murphy	D Cronin
K Moseley	A Reed
M Roderick	L Dallaglio
J Irons	M White
I Morgan	C Sheasby

Scorers
West Hartlepool. Tries: C John, Peacock, Botham. Penalties: C John (2). Conversion: C John.
Wasps. Tries: King, Gomarsall, Sheasby, White, Mitchell, Henderson, penalty try. Penalties: Rees (5). Conversions: Rees (5).

Replacements
West Hartlepool: W de Jonge replaced by D Barnes (59 minutes), M Roderick replaced by A McKennedy (24).
Wasps: A King replaced by M Wood (63), A Gomarsall replaced by R McKinsey (77), M White replaced by D Macer (65).

15 FEBRUARY 1997

Five Nations' Championship: Ireland 6 England 46

I was one of the players, along with Richard Hill and a number of others, who had been to Dublin before and played at Donnybrook for the A team. Although many of us had some experience of playing representative rugby in Ireland it doesn't prepare you for the size and magnitude of the Five Nations' game. That is a different matter altogether.

People were saying that the Irish played badly against

France but Brian Ashton of Bath fame had now assumed control of the team. It was being built up as a battle of the two Bath men, Ashton v. Rowell. But for us that was never really on the agenda, it was about England v. Ireland. Jason Leonard gave the team talk. He's played many times in Dublin and he warned us that from the moment we arrived, they would be laughing, joking, smiling and patting us on the back, telling us how good we are, that we are going to beat them by twenty points and we shouldn't really be on the same field. They are so welcoming that you are almost taken in by it – you forget that you're out there to play a very hard rugby match. Jason told us to prepare for this and to remain very tough and focused, and I think that was the key.

I think only five of the starting line-up had played in Dublin before, but perhaps that was to our advantage. I've never lost to Ireland at any international level, so I didn't take any emotional baggage with me. In years gone by you'd know a few of the Irish team, because a lot of them would be playing club rugby in England, but there would still be guys who had never really been seen in England previously. Therefore it was always difficult to get a true value of their abilities. However, in these modern professional times nearly the entire squad play club rugby in England, which was lucky for me because it was my job to analyse the opposition. It's a thing we do called 'Knowing the Enemy' – you list the opposition, what their strengths and weaknesses are and how you think they'll play individually. Obviously, it's important to collate information from the rest of the team. For example, Carling and Leonard would know more about Jim Staples than I would – they play with him at Harlequins every week. Getting an idea of the opposition does help, there's no doubt about that, but we don't over-focus on them – we also look at the details of our own performance. Jack Rowell doesn't leave any stone unturned and so you feel as if you are fully prepared.

We arrived there on the Thursday; the weather was good and I was getting a bit worried that we had got the timing wrong – I know the sun only shines once in every five days there. I wished it was match day because we would have loved to play in this weather. But this was Thursday, and the weather was due to get progressively worse. However, when I woke up on the day of the match it was a beautiful sunny day. It was quite a surreal feeling – all the talk had been about the storm we were going to face and the gale force winds and the hurricane, weather that usually goes with an international in Ireland. It just seemed very unusual but I knew that if it stayed like that for the rest of the day, we would play well.

The build-up to the game on the day of the match was interesting – for me it was like a throwback to the old days. People had talked about the atmosphere at Lansdowne Road and I found it much more akin to what you would expect from rugby, with the crowds very close to the touchline. This is no modern hi-tech stadium, but it certainly provides an intimate and genuine rugby atmosphere, the sort I remember experiencing when I was standing on the terraces of the old Twickenham.

Ireland kicked off and started with the usual frantic, frenetic kick and chase. Eric Elwood was putting kicks up, they were trying to rattle a few cages and it got a bit punchy early on – it was everything that we expected. We expected that to go on for the whole match, but in actual fact it seemed to subside. They weren't without their problems – Elwood was wincing in pain from a knee injury, which he had sustained in a club match the week before, and it was clearly affecting his kicking. He was off target with a couple of penalties, his restarts weren't as good as they usually are and it wasn't long before he was off the pitch. The Eric Miller incident had an effect because he was the one player in their pack who posed a genuine threat, one which we had worked very hard on defending. There was nothing malicious about the incident, he just landed the wrong way in a tackle and ended up getting a few heavyweights falling on top of him – and that ended his game. Along with those two going off went Ireland's chance of keeping sustained pressure on England.

We started to take control, we took the ball up field and we got the first try. Jon Sleightholme took his man on, one on one, and beat him for pace, plain and simple. I half expected Ireland to come right back into it. If we could win the game in the first twenty minutes and then pile on the points for the rest of the game then we would do. But there seemed to be a pattern emerging – we were taking a while to break sides down and then letting rip with a barrage of points. That wasn't the game plan here; the plan was to play for eighty-five minutes and to give Ireland respect. Defences are tight initially, guys are pumped up and they're knocking people down. As the game goes on and people start to get tired, both in defence and attack, that's when the gaps start appearing. Once we did get the opportunities to score, we took them.

There were some very promising things to come out of the Ireland game – the pack had once again stamped their authority on the game and the back row had a much better balance. I thought Rodber and Hill had their best games for England so far. A lot of people had criticised Tim for going to ground too early, saying that he should take people on, drive the ball forward and give the forwards a target to ruck over. Leading up to the game the Press had asked if Tim was the right man for the job at No. 8 and said he hadn't played well since South Africa in 1994. That motivated him to play a belter, and he did play well. We finished the game off in style. It was nice to see Guscott and Healey brought on, although it's easy to make substitutions when you're thirty points up. When you introduce new players at a time in the game when everyone else is physically wearing out, fresh legs make an immediate impression – and those two did just that. Healey had a little dart and set up the pass for Hill's try and every time Jerry touched the ball he seemed to do something positive with it, he put Tony Underwood in twice. They must have been pleased because they only had five minutes to show their skills, but they were involved in

England's most productive period of the match. Some of the passages of play epitomised the sort of rugby that we want to play – to keep ball and keep recycling it until gaps appear and then exploit them. We were particularly pleased and there's no doubt that we had a cracking night celebrating. Dublin is a great place to go at any time, but when you win a Five Nations' match with a record score it is even better. People were picking bits out of the performance and saying that we could improve, but we had now scored eighty-seven points in two Five Nations' games, had two record victories and were in good shape for the game against France.

Ireland 6 England 46

Ireland	*England*
J Staples (Harlequins)	T Stimpson (Newcastle)
D Hickie (St Mary's College)	J Sleightholme (Bath)
J Bell (Northampton)	W Carling (Harlequins)
M Field (Malone)	P de Glanville (Bath)
J Topping (Ballymena)	T Underwood (Newcastle)
E Elwood (Lansdowne)	P Grayson (Northampton)
N Hogan (Terenure College)	A Gomarsall (Wasps)
N Popplewell (Newcastle)	G Rowntree (Leicester)
R Nesdale (Newcastle)	M Regan (Bristol)
P Wallace (Saracens)	J Leonard (Harlequins)
D Corkery (Bristol)	L Dallaglio (Wasps)
P Johns (Saracens)	M Johnson (Leicester)
J Davidson (London Irish)	S Shaw (Bristol)
W McBride (Malone)	R Hill (Saracens)
E Miller (Leicester)	T Rodber (Northampton)

Scorers
Ireland. Penalties: Elwood (2).
England. Tries: Sleightholme (2), Underwood (2), Gomarsall, Hill. Penalties: Grayson (4). Conversions: Grayson (2).

Replacements
Ireland: E Miller replaced by A Foley (Shannon; 12 minutes), E Elwood replaced by D Humphreys (London Irish; 25), N Hogan replaced by B O'Meara (Cork Constitution; 66).
England: A Gomarsall replaced by A Healey (Leicester; 74), W Carling replaced by J Guscott (Bath; 77).

23 FEBRUARY 1997

Courage League Division One: Wasps 36
West Hartlepool 12

This was a rearranged game. West Hartlepool had cancelled the original fixture (which was to have been played on 30 October) because they could not put out a reasonable front row. This had worried me slightly as it seemed that clubs were making a mockery of the league rules. If you can't make a front row then you should borrow one from somewhere. As it happened, things probably worked out well for us. When you play a side twice in two consecutive weeks, beating them heavily the first time never suggests that you will do the same thing the second time. The team that has won can get carried away and the beaten team think they will make sure that they put up a bit more of a fight.

The game was played in a very sombre atmosphere on a Sunday at Sudbury. We scored six tries and won the game with a reasonably good performance. We were now well into the second half of the league campaign and had only lost two matches. We were not racking up century scorelines, but we were doing a good job, averaging a fairly impressive thirty-one points per game

Wasps 36 West Hartlepool 12

Wasps	*West Hartlepool*
G Rees	M Silva
J Ufton	M Wood
N Greenstock	L Botham
R Henderson	J Connolly
S Roiser	S John
G Gregory	C John
A Gomarsall	M Roderick
D Molloy	D Barnes
S Mitchell	M Kennedy
W Green	W de Jonge
D Cronin	C Murphy
A Reed	L Francis

Diary of a Season

L Dallaglio	J Irons
M White	M Emerson
C Sheasby	I Morgan

Scorers
Wasps. Tries: Rees, Ufton, Gregory, Sheasby, Reed, penalty try.
Conversions: Rees (3).
West Hartlepool. Tries: S John (2). Conversion: C John.

Replacements
Wasps: S Mitchell was replaced by K Dunn, D Molloy was replaced by
I Dunston.

7 Grand Slam Disappointment

1 MARCH 1997

Five Nations' Championship: England 20 France 23

France had played very well leading up to the England game. They had beaten Ireland away from home and had run out winners in a tough game against Wales in Cardiff. But this was the key game of the tournament and everyone was looking forward to it.

Last season we won every match apart from the French game, and that cost us the Grand Slam. This time we were very, very confident but we had to sprinkle that confidence with a bit of common sense and realise that the quality of the opposition meant that we could expect a really tough game. For France to beat us they would have to put together a pretty special performance because we felt that home advantage would give us an edge.

We were able to put the same side out, which was good news. People were growing accustomed to playing with each other and had real confidence. But there certainly wasn't any over-confidence. We've had some real ding dong battles with France in the past and just because we had scored eighty-odd points in the last two games didn't mean that we were going to steamroller France. But we were certainly feeling strong and confident in our own abilities. The French camp had heavily involved Pierre Villepreux who played down France's chances by saying that we were a formidable team. Perhaps it was a little bit of kidology on his part. Our preparation was ideal. We looked at the areas where we felt we could break them down – we felt that, physically, we had an edge up front and that, defensively, if we could knock them down we could then impose our rhythm and style on them and really get going. The important thing was to get the crowd behind us, get some early scores and start playing with the sort of authority that we knew we could produce.

The referee, Jim Fleming, seemed to blow his whistle quite a bit – there seemed to be a lot of infringements. In the first scrum we got caught a bit cold and ended up giving away a penalty. Lamaison kicked it and they took a three-point lead. From then on, it was all England. We played exceptionally well, we put a lot of phases of play together, we played a controlled game, we varied tactics nicely, we box kicked, we ran with the ball, we threw miss moves and we recycled possession. We really took the game to them but got only penalties as a reward for our efforts. Just before half time we made a break down the left-hand side, Graham Rowntree took it in on the burst and, as I was getting off the floor Phil de Glanville took the ball on. I called from a very deep position – I think that the depth of my position was perhaps the one thing that caught them off guard – and Phil played a superb inside pass. He definitely heard my call and I hit it at pace. It's very easy at pace when you are coming from deep because your momentum takes you through a gap before anyone can do anything about it. Once I'd beaten Abdel Benazzi on the left-hand side there was only one way I was going to go, and that was straight through to the line. That was a fantastic feeling, me and the crowd against a couple of French defenders, and with the adrenalin running through my system, it would have taken someone pretty quick to have stopped me. It was a great time to score, just before half time. France had defended quite well and must have been disappointed to go into the break 14–6 down. The try gave us just the sort of lift we needed. I was delighted.

There was no complacency at the half-time team talk. We

knew that we were going to have to work hard for another forty-five minutes but we felt that we had a chance to really cut loose and perhaps produce something pretty special. We started the second half by taking them on and we ended up getting a couple of penalties for our efforts. Ironically, those two penalties ended up being the only two times we actually got in their half. But at the time it was going better than anyone could have imagined. We were ten minutes into the second half and we were 20–6 up against a very good French side. Then, all of a sudden, things began to go wrong. We lost a little bit of discipline, our kickoffs were going deep and Olivier Merle, who had been having a very quiet game suddenly gained a bit of inspiration. He was making good two handed catches and the French pack were getting round him and driving him forward. Then we started to give away a few penalties and indiscipline crept into the team while the French worked their way up field. They kicked a penalty and we kicked off with a poor kick that went deep to Merle – we just seemed to be playing right into their hands.

All we needed to do was get our hands on the ball so that we could work our way back up field and get some more points but everything we did seemed to go wrong. From broken play we would win ball and then kick it to Jean-Luc Sadourny, straight down his throat. When you have a player of his calibre you would be lucky to get away with that once or twice but when you kick it straight at him five or six times, he's definitely going to make you pay for it. That really put pressure on us. The pace of the game for the first fifty minutes had been far different to any other previous Five Nations' match and it was having an effect on both sides. Benazzi was injured and France were forced to make a double substitution. It gave them a lift to have fresh legs on the pitch, and those guys came on and started driving the ball close and tight, right into the heart of us. We found it difficult to cope with the new enthusiasm, the new momentum that was being created by just a couple of players. We needed to calm things down, but it's very difficult to put the brakes on that sort of momentum.

The reason we lost the game was a culmination of a number of things. The half backs would be the first to say that we kicked ball away. Instead of finding the spaces in the field or touch, we were finding a blue shirt and they were coming back at us. I think at half time the French were dead and buried but, as they started to hit their best form, they could feel that we were waning.

We called a line-out and it was slow. The throw wasn't right, the jump wasn't right. It just clipped the top of Martin Johnson's hand and went right over the back, and France secured the ball. From that came a carbon copy of the try they scored against Wales and that infuriated me. It was a typical French try, a chip over the top with Leflamand beating Underwood to the ball and scoring. To have let them in with such a cheap try like that was frustrating and panic was definitely setting in. We needed to relax and get things back on track, think to ourselves that we were still 20–13 up. But Merle caught the kickoff again, the French forwards came back at us and we gave another penalty away.

We should have made some substitutions. I looked round the pitch and there were guys limping, and we had quality players like Ben Clarke and Jerry Guscott on the bench. It would have given us a chance to get some instructions from the bench and some fresh legs on at a time when clearly some of the guys were struggling, but for one reason or another we did not decide to do that. I had the same feeling that I had when we were playing the New Zealand Barbarians where we were winning but they were coming back at us and finishing the stronger team. Then they got the line-out right down our right-hand side of the South Stand. They secured the ball, took it in field, took it on again, reversed it very quickly and scored another try. After all our hard work I could not believe that we had allowed them to come back. It was just incredible. We had got ourselves into a position where we could have killed them off and finished the game running out comfortable winners, but we let them right back in.

I felt we had lost control of our own performance and, as well as France played, they really just did what was required. They kept their heads under pressure and we lost ours at a time when we were not under any pressure. But now it was 20–20 and we thought we could still win. Again the kickoff was a poor one – it came right back at us. I was adjudged to have given away the penalty that lost us the match. I felt that I was on my feet and still believe that their guy came in on a crash ball, went down and held on to it. I was bent over trying to pull the ball off when the rest of our team came in and a pile-up formed. Fleming gave the penalty against us. I thought that, if anything, it was a penalty to us. I was deeply disappointed and, of course, Lamaison kept a cool head and put the kick over.

Then, in the last five minutes we started playing with the sort of urgency that had been lacking in the last twenty. We were just running from anywhere and taking them on. I think that we've got to play like that for the whole game and not just try to shut up shop when we are winning. The feeling in the dressing room was one of total shock and there was a deadly silence. It was deeply depressing to have played so well for half an hour and then to have blown everything by losing the mental focus and letting the skill level drop for a split second to let them back in the game.

England 20 France 23

England
T Stimpson (Newcastle)
J Sleightholme (Bath)
W Carling (Harlequins)
P de Glanville (Bath)
T Underwood (Newcastle)
P Grayson (Northampton)
A Gomarsall (Wasps)
G Rowntree (Leicester)
M Regan (Bristol)
J Leonard (Harlequins)
L Dallaglio (Wasps)

France
J-L Sadourny (Colomiers)
L Leflamand (Bourgoin)
C Lamaison (Brive)
S Glas (Bourgoin)
D Venditti (Brive)
A Penaud (Brive)
P Carbonneau (Brive)
C Califano (Toulouse)
M Dalmaso (Agen)
F Tournaire (Narbonne)
A Benazzi (Agen)

M Johnson (Leicester)
S Shaw (Bristol)
R Hill (Saracens)
T Rodber (Northampton)

O Merle (Montferrand)
H Miorin (Toulouse)
O Magne (Dax)
F Pelous (Dax)

Scorers
England. Try: Dallaglio. Penalties: Grayson (4). Dropped goal: Grayson.
France. Tries: Leflamand, Lamaison. Penalties: Lamaison (2). Conversions: Lamaison (2). Dropped goal: Lamaison.

Replacements
France: A Benazzi replaced by M de Rougemont (Toulon; 65).

15 MARCH 1997

Five Nations' Championship: Wales 13 England 34

We had lost the French game; the chance of winning the Grand Slam and the Five Nations' had gone, and therefore the pressure was off. But someone was going to have to pay the price for a poor result against France, so Healey came in at scrum-half. Gomarsall took the blame for a lot of the things that went wrong but I think that the responsibility was a collective one and it was unfortunate that he had to take a bit more of the blame than perhaps he should have done. I don't think that the management wanted to change the team too much. They felt that the players had let themselves down against France and needed to be given a collective opportunity to put that right.

Our attitude towards the style of play had definitely changed during the season. Before, we played a style of rugby which was going to win us games but wasn't going to win us the World Cup. People now genuinely wanted to run and play a fifteen-man game but I think there was a danger that we would revert to type in order to win the game against Wales. For so many seasons England had got so bogged down in the rivalry between the home unions that they sacrificed style in order to get the result. People didn't seem to care if we went down to Cardiff and won by only a point. But hard lessons have now been learnt from the

World Cup – we had left England as supposedly the best side in the northern hemisphere but we came back with our tails between our legs.

When we met up after the French game, there were a lot of tired bodies because we had had league games in between (Wasps had beaten Gloucester 36–10). We split up as forwards and backs and had a very honest and open discussion about where we felt we played well and where the positives were and, more importantly, where we felt we had let ourselves down and why we had lost the game. How did we let them back into it? The general feeling was that we should approach the Wales game exactly how we had approached the other three games. We needed to go down there and impose our rhythm and style on the Welsh and make sure that we got a result. There was a feeling of 'let's go out there and prove to all that France was just a one-off.' We knew that if we didn't beat Wales, the season would be remembered for the bad twenty minutes we played against France. Before England's win in Cardiff under Will Carling in 1991 the last time we had won there was in 1963 when my ex-schoolmaster John Willcox was in the side.

The build-up to the Welsh game was not without its problems and I had a lot of things going on in my head. Alice was due to give birth on 11 March – four days before the game – and that was the most important thing on my mind. It was not something I had discussed in great detail with Jack Rowell. He knew that we were expecting a baby, and the date, but it wasn't something that I allowed myself to panic about openly; but deep down, I was concerned. I was also thinking about the prospect of going to Hong Kong on the Monday. I had been appointed captain of the England team for the World Cup Sevens. To go there as holders of the trophy and to play in another World Cup Sevens was a huge honour for me, and I accepted it without really thinking about what else was going on at the same time. I had confused the expected date of birth with the date I was due to fly out to Hong Kong, otherwise I would not have made that decision. But I don't like to let anyone down, I say yes to everyone and think about the consequences later – it's not a good habit, it's just the way I am.

I was now starting to get excited, worried and emotional about the pregnancy. I was also thinking about the Sevens and the prospect of going to Hong Kong, while at the same time trying to keep myself focused on the Wales game. I was also thinking about Alice because I had been away from home every other week for the last six weeks, so I had not seen a great deal of her. I had been coming back from an international match, sorting the bags out for two or three days and then going to a hotel again. Generally everything seemed to be happening at one hundred miles per hour, and I was just trying to keep things together and stay calm. The Press were now starting to discuss my domestic and rugby priorities. If I was given the situation all over again I might act differently, but at the time it was hard to make decisions because I hardly had time to think, there was so much going on. I thought that if I had to rush home from Cardiff to be at the birth and share the joys of parenthood with Alice then I would do that, and then rush back and score the winning try – I could not see a problem really.

The first thing that happened in training for the Wales game was that Paul Grayson got injured. As much as I like Paul and as well as he had been playing, I was not worried about the fact that he had got injured. I thought it would be the ideal opportunity to give Alex King a chance to play in the game. The Grand Slam opportunity had gone so it was a good time to put him in and see what he could do. But by the Wednesday before the game, when it became apparent that Paul wasn't going to play, the rumour was that Rob Andrew was coming down to join the squad.

The counter-rumour was that either Mike Catt or Alex would play. I thought that Alex would be given the opportunity because he had been sitting on the bench while Mike played fly half for three games. When it was heard that

Rob was coming down we thought it might just be to get involved as a coach or something like that. When he arrived Jason Leonard and Will Carling gave him the usual welcome. He had obviously been very heavily involved in Newcastle but he had answered an SOS call to come down. It soon became very clear that Mike Catt would come in while Rob sat on the bench. Alex King was taken to one side and told what was happening; he was very disappointed not to be playing. He had not been given any opportunity to perform, he was the only guy in the squad that had not been capped, and had been playing very well for a winning Wasps side. To top it all, he was now being overlooked for someone who had clearly stated that he did not want to be involved in international rugby.

Rob Andrew has been a wonderful player and he taught me a lot about the mental approach to the game. I will never forget when England dropped him in favour of Stuart Barnes. As he had already played forty-one times for England, people thought that it might be the end of his international career. It turned out that being dropped made Rob even more determined. He was the last guy in from training every day that week and he became more and more determined to get his place back in the team. That showed me how mentally hard this guy was. He did get his place back in the team and went on to win more caps for England and he has been responsible for much of England's success. As a player he has done it all, but when he retired from international rugby I did not think that he would come back in any way or form. Realistically, Rob Andrew will never be the next fly half to lead England to the next World Cup – Alex King or Mike Catt is more likely to – and, as we had already lost the Five Nations' Championship, the Wales game was an ideal time to give others a chance.

Wales were ravaged by injury. The absence of Scott Gibbs was a huge blow – he had been the inspiration for their tackling – and Ieuan Evans was out as well. Most of the players they looked to for a lead were missing and I think that had an effect on them. On the other hand, it was going to be the last game at the Cardiff ground, it was going to be Jonathan Davies' last game, and it was against England, so all of the Welsh squad was certainly fired up for it.

We trained on Wednesday and I was clearly coming down with something, I felt drained during the training session, I had not been sleeping well all week, I was starting to feel hot and I was getting a temperature. The last time I was ill I was at school. I don't get ill, I don't attract illnesses as other people do – I fight them off and get on with the job. But I was feeling more and more unwell. The build-up to the game, anxiety about Alice and the baby and the worry about going away to Hong Kong for the week all added up to intense strain, and it was taking its toll on me. I spoke to Terry Crystal, the team doctor. Terry and Kevin Murphy, the physiotherapist, knew me well enough to realise that I don't go to see them unless there's a real problem. At this stage it was not too much to worry about, it was only Wednesday. Terry gave me some tablets to try and bring the temperature down. But when we trained on Thursday morning I felt that my condition was deteriorating rapidly. The plan was to drive our cars to Bristol, leave them, and get the coach over to Cardiff. I felt so weak on Thursday afternoon that I had to get Ben Clarke to drive my car. I was beginning to worry – this was Thursday and I had a huge international match on the Saturday. I had lost my appetite and I was starting to feel very bad indeed. I lay in silence on the bus all the way to Cardiff. I awoke in Cardiff to find that my head was throbbing and I was burning up. Terry had phoned ahead to Cardiff and made arrangements to keep me away from the rest of the squad. By now I felt so weak that I couldn't do anything but lie in bed and, when I woke up on Friday, I had an incredibly sore throat. I was getting early signs of tonsillitis and I told Terry that we ought to inform Jack of the situation.

Terry came back and told me that Jack was prepared to give me until Saturday morning to make a decision. On

Friday afternoon I started to feel a little better. Half of me really wanted to play and finish the season on a huge high, the other half, the common sense half, said, 'You've worked incredibly hard this season with Wasps and England; you may be on the verge of being picked for the British Lions; you really do not want to mess it all up in the last game because at the end of the day people only remember your last performance.' It reminded me of the time when I had just broken into the Wasps team. I played with flu and had one of the worst games of my life. I was dropped after that game and it taught me a very harsh lesson – that you don't put yourself out on the pitch unless you can do yourself justice. I was thinking of going out to an international at Cardiff and trying to play when I couldn't even stand up straight without feeling weak. I was also thinking about Alice and how I could do with being at home with her. I was speaking to her regularly; she knew my condition and I knew hers – we were both bedridden. I was on the phone to her all the time. She didn't want to stop me from playing for England, she wanted me to go to Hong Kong and she also wanted me to be there at the birth. It was now obvious that I wouldn't be able to do all three. I made the decision that I wasn't well enough to play and Jack Rowell was informed. I was very disappointed but I knew it was the right decision. Jack came up to the room at about half past twelve and said that he too was disappointed and that he thought that I had come on a hell of a lot this season for England, that I was an important part of the team but the most important thing was that I get myself right and back on track. A lot of the guys had phoned me up to commiserate and I was grateful for their support.

Ben Clarke was brought in to replace me. It says a lot about England's strength in depth that they could bring a player of his ability in. Ben said that he was disappointed for me, that he would have liked me to play but also that he would make sure that he went out there and played well. He did a good job.

I was relieved I had made a decision. So, at the same time, I made the decision not to go to Hong Kong as well. I hadn't eaten for three days at this stage, and Terry said that I would be in no state to play by Thursday or Friday. I spoke to Les Cusworth, the coach for the Sevens, and said that it had been a very difficult decision for me to make but that I wouldn't be able to do the team justice. Richard Hill had been left out of the squad so I knew there was a very capable replacement waiting in the wings. Then I spoke to Alice and said, 'Look, you haven't had the baby yet and I'm not going out to Hong Kong.' She was overwhelmed by that decision, and relieved that I would be coming home on Saturday night.

I wanted us to go out and stuff the Welsh. It was quite an unusual feeling to watch a game on television but I couldn't have gone to the ground in my condition. The first half was quite scrappy and we were only just ahead, then we really cut loose and performed well. Catt had a superb game as did Hill. Ben came in and played well at blind side on my behalf. It was nice for Sheasby to get a Five Nations' cap, and Darren Garforth was capped as well. But there was concern for Mark Regan who was stretchered off. It looked ominous but it turned out that he had only twisted his ankle ligaments. Jerry Guscott again came on as a substitute, and again made a huge impression. We absorbed everything that they threw at us and came out comfortable winners. The turning point was the interception try by Tony Underwood which gave us the confidence to cut loose and score some super tries. To go and beat Wales at Cardiff, and in the given circumstances, was a great achievement.

Wales 13 England 34

Wales	*England*
N Jenkins (Pontypridd)	T Stimpson (Newcastle)
S Hill (Cardiff)	J Sleightholme (Bath)
A Bateman (Richmond)	W Carling (Harlequins)
N Davies (Llanelli)	P de Glanville (Bath)
G Thomas (Bridgend)	T Underwood (Newcastle)

J Davies (Cardiff)	M Catt (Bath)
R Howley (Cardiff)	A Healey (Leicester)
C Loader (Swansea)	G Rowntree (Leicester)
J Humphreys (Cardiff)	M Regan (Bristol)
D Young (Cardiff)	J Leonard (Harlequins)
S Williams (Neath)	B Clarke (Richmond)
G Llewellyn (Harlequins)	M Johnson (Leicester)
M Voyle (Llanelli)	S Shaw (Bristol)
K Jones (Ebbw Vale)	R Hill (Saracens)
L Quinnell (Richmond)	T Rodber (Northampton)

Scorers
Wales. Try: Howley. Penalties: J Davies. Conversion: J Davies.
England. Tries: Stimpson, Underwood, Hill, de Glanville. Penalties: Catt (2). Conversions: Catt (4).

Replacements
Wales. C Loader replaced by S John (Llanelli; 23), K Jones replaced by D McIntosh (Pontypridd; 65), M Voyle replaced by J Quinnell (Richmond; 69).
England. J Sleightholme replaced by J Guscott (Bath; 41), B Clarke replaced by C Sheasby (Wasps; 70), M Catt replaced by R Andrew (Newcastle; 73), G Rowntree replaced by D Garforth (Leicester; 78).

Afterwards I felt really bad. My car was in Bristol, I was in Cardiff and the Sevens guys were about to leave to go back to London. Tim Rodber was to give me a lift to Bristol so I could drive back home to London from there. We made a pretty sharp exit from Cardiff with Richard Hill also in the car. It was a huge relief to me. I just wanted to get home and get away from what had been a nightmare week. The next few days I spent recovering. I was still on the antibiotics, I was still bedridden, I wasn't taking much food and it was not until Wednesday that I started to feel a bit better.

By now the baby was six days overdue. Wednesday went fairly normally and I decided to cook some food in the evening for us. It was the first time that I had done any cooking for ages. Alice had been having contractions all day, but they had been quite few and far between. But just as I was making an incredible mess in the kitchen she started to go into labour, experiencing some quite heavy contractions.

I left the kitchen like a bomb had hit it and we drove off to the hospital. There is always the fear that you have gone too early and you will be told to go home or to sit in the labour ward until things start happening. But Alice was well into labour and, although she said that she would like to go home and chill out, the hospital decided to hang on to her.

It was quite funny because a new midwife came on duty and informed Alice that, although she was three centimetres dilated and could expect to continue dilating at one centimetre an hour, she would not give birth until she reached ten centimetres. The birth was not imminent after all and I wished that I had brought a pillow because it seemed that we were going to be there a while. Eventually, I thought that I would go and get a bit of sleep on the bed, so I put my head down for an hour or so – all the girls outside had been telling the midwife that I was a rugby player and she said that I needed to keep my strength up. She brought me breakfast at 5 a.m. and made me cups of coffee, which was very nice of her and much appreciated. Alice said she wasn't going to have any epidurals or any drugs of any description but she ended up having gas and air, which I confess to having a little bit of myself. It got to 8 a.m. and she was now ten centimetres dilated. We had been in hospital for about ten hours. Alice expected the baby just to drop out at that stage but she had some pushing to do first. Ella was born at 10.07 a.m. on Thursday morning. Alice hadn't eaten all night so I was doing what any rugby player would do, I was chucking energy tablets in her mouth and feeding her high-energy drinks.

I was just so pleased that I was there all the way through, and Alice actually ended up leaning on me as Ella Francesca was born. It was an incredible experience and one that I would not have missed for the world. I didn't even know if it was a boy or girl for about ten minutes after the birth – I was so excited, happy, and emotional that I forgot to look. Apparently, our lovely little girl had been in a posterior position for quite some time and had obviously been causing Alice some pain. I thought that Alice was incredibly brave to push her out without any epidurals or drugs. Ella weighed 9.5 lb at birth so she was one huge girl. Someone up above was looking after us – it was a hell of a day that ended with the best possible result.

The league situation in March was encouraging, with three home games – a major plus with the critical part of the season approaching. Gloucester came first and this was a chance to set the record straight after losing at Kingsholm earlier in the season, a result which still irritated. Kenny Logan, who had been playing up in Scotland for Stirling County, made his debut in this match. He had been to have a look at us both in play and in training. He liked what he saw and signed. So we now had an international wing in our ranks for the finishing run. Essentially, Kenny had moved in order to play with better players. The bonus was that, socially, he fitted in well from the minute he arrived.

9 MARCH 1997

Courage League Division One: Wasps 36 Gloucester 10

Gloucester gave us a little concern because they managed to put some pressure on. They scored a try and it was some time before we felt we were in a winning groove and were able to open up in the way we wanted. But we finished up scoring three tries and winning 36–10.

Wasps 36 Gloucester 10

Wasps	*Gloucester*
G Rees	C Catling
S Roiser	M Peters
N Greenstock	D Caskie
R Henderson	M Roberts
K Logan	M Lloyd
A King	M Mapletoft
A Gomarsall	S Benton
D Molloy	A Windo

S Mitchell	P Greening
W Green	A Deacon
L Dallaglio	P Glanville
D Cronin	R Fidler
A Reed	D Sims
M White	N Carter
C Sheasby	S Devereux

Scorers
Wasps. Tries: King, Greenstock, Roiser. Penalties: Rees (5). Conversions: Rees (3).
Gloucester. Try: Catling. Penalty: Mapletoft. Conversion: Mapletoft.

Replacements
Wasps: D Cronin replaced by M Greenwood (6 minutes), K Logan replaced by J Ufton (79).
Gloucester: S Benton replaced by L Beck (40), M Mapletoft replaced by M Kimber (60), A Deacon replaced by P Vickery (60), N Carter replaced by A Stanley (60).

22 MARCH 1997

Courage League Division One: Wasps 62 Orrell 5

The Orrell game was at Sudbury and, as it looked fairly certain that we would not be playing there again there was a fair amount of nostalgia attached to the game. It really meant something to those who had been playing at Sudbury for a year or two. We had a very big first half but then went back a gear or two in the second. You just never know how important points difference might be later on so we were trying to score as many tries as possible. We finished up with nine, something we had achieved just once before, against Toulouse. Kenny Logan scored five, a league record, and did just the finishing job we knew he could.

Wasps 62 Orrell 5

Wasps	*Orrell*
G Rees	S Taberner
S Roiser	J Naylor
N Greenstock	L Tuigamala
R Henderson	D Lyon

K Logan	N Heslop
A King	M McCarthy
A Gomarsall	S Cook
D Molloy	M Worsley
S Mitchell	N Hitchin
W Green	S Turner
M Greenwood	P Rees
A Reed	C Cusani
L Dallaglio	P Angelsea
M White	R Higgs
P Scrivener	A Bennett

Scorers
Wasps. Tries: Logan (5), Greenstock, Scrivener, Roiser. Penalty: Rees.
Conversions: Rees (6).
Orrell. Try: Heslop.

Replacements
Wasps: G Rees replaced by J Ufton (62 minutes), S Mitchell replaced by
K Dunn (62), A Reed replaced by R Kinsey (63), A Gomarsall
temporarily replaced by M Wood (59–62).
Orrell: S Taberner replaced by W Munroe (74), L Tuigamala replaced
by P Hamer (34), N Hitchin replaced by A Moffatt (36), P Rees replaced
by C Brierly (74).

27 MARCH 1997

Courage League Division One: Wasps 31 London Irish 18

London Irish were scrapping for everything they could get at
this stage of the season and came at us with all guns firing. It
turned out to be a very ill-tempered match with fracas
breaking out every so often. I knew that having squeezed
through at Sudbury earlier in the season that this one might
be difficult. We made it harder for ourselves with a few
unforced errors but we managed to come out winners. It was
a difficult job well done under the floodlights of Loftus Road.

Wasps 31 London Irish 18
Wasps	*London Irish*
G Rees	C O'Shea
S Roiser	J Bishop

Diary of a Season

N Greenstock
R Henderson
K Logan
A King
A Gomarsall
D Molloy
S Mitchell
W Green
L Dallaglio
M Greenwood
A Reed
M White
P Scrivener

P Flood
N Burrows
R Hennessy
S Burns
N Hogan
J Fitzpatrick
A Redmond
G Halpin
K O'Connell
G Fulcher
J Davidson
C Bird
R Yeabsley

Scorers
Wasps. Tries: Greenstock, penalty tries (2). Penalties: Rees (2). Conversions: Rees (2). Dropped goal: King.
London Irish. Tries: Flood, Fulcher. Penalties: O'Shea (2). Conversion: O'Shea.

Replacements
Wasps: S Roiser replaced by J Ufton (71 minutes), M White replaced by P Volley (82).
London Irish: J Bishop replaced by A Allen (55).

8 Taking the Title

2 APRIL 1997

Courage League Division One: Leicester 18 Wasps 12

Wednesday 2 April 1997 was one of the most significant days of the season. The team for the British Lions tour to South Africa was to be announced in the morning. And in the evening Wasps were to play Leicester – a mammoth game.

I get apprehensive before any selection but the Lions was the big one, the biggest for any player in Britain or Ireland. The Lions drip with history and whoever was selected would become part of that history. I was excited at the prospect and, whether I was involved or not, it was going to be interesting to see how the squad of thirty-six players would be structured. The names were coming out on Sky TV although I actually heard the news via Radio 5 Live. On hearing my name my reaction was one of relief, excitement and pride – I realised that I was at the pinnacle of the game. I knew there was no greater honour, and as the names of the players went round in my head, I realised that the Lions had chosen a squad for the job, simply going for the players that they believed could do the business in South Africa. One of my first thoughts was that I was pleased that I had already been to South Africa with England. I felt that the experience I had gained in 1994 would be invaluable.

I counted up the Leicester players in the squad and found that they had six, including the Lions captain Martin Johnson. I did wonder for a while whether Leicester might be diverted from the task later that day because of all the excitement over the Lions. I was excited enough on my own. What would a group of six be thinking as Leicester counted down to that league match? But I knew I would have to pull myself in and focus on the match at hand.

Leicester had gone to town for the game. There was additional seating, taking the crowd up to 18,000. You could feel the buzz the moment you stepped into the ground. I felt we were well organised, and, as a team, we knew how we could win, how we could defend and how we could implement our game plan. There was real awareness in our camp but I am sure that the Tigers, with their six Lions, had prepared just as thoroughly.

The match did not let anyone down and, defensively, it was the best game we played. It was also the toughest game of the season and Leicester probably felt the same. We had two try-scoring opportunities which went astray, one of them when Alex King make an outside break but passed inside to Neil Back. It was our first league defeat since the Harlequins game in January. But that same night we heard that Bath had been beaten at Sale. As we were playing them the following Sunday at Loftus Road, there was considerable debate about what the results meant for both of us. Apparently, Phil de Glanville said that Bath were out of it but I would not have gone so far.

Leicester 18 Wasps 12

Leicester	*Wasps*
N Malone	G Rees
S Hackney	S Roiser
W Greenwood	N Greenstock
C Joiner	R Henderson
L Lloyd	K Logan
J Stransky	A King
A Healey	A Gomarsall
G Rowntree	D Molloy
R Cockerill	S Mitchell
D Garforth	W Green

M Johnson	M Greenwood
M Poole	A Reed
E Miller	L Dallaglio
N Back	M White
D Richards	C Sheasby

Scorers
Leicester. Penalties: Stransky (6).
Wasps. Penalties: Rees (4)

Replacements
Leicester: L Lloyd replaced by R Underwood (65 minutes), A Healey replaced by A Kardooni (76).
Wasps: S Mitchell replaced by K Dunn (48).

6 APRIL 1997

Courage League Division One: Wasps 25 Bath 25

Wasps v. Bath was a mouth-watering prospect, especially as the 40–36 score we had over them in September had stayed fresh in our minds. I think it fair to say that no one was disappointed by the outcome. Wasps were a bit of a mixture: sometimes we were at our best, at other times we had lapses in concentration which cost us dearly. It was 6–6 and approaching half time when we gave away a penalty in front of the posts. Mike Catt approached the mark as if he was going to take a kick at goal but instead he took a quick tap, set it off on the blind side, and Jerry Guscott scored. Not long after that Guscott sent Adebayo clear with a neat pass and we were starting to wonder if we could ever get back into the game.

Gareth Rees helped to stabilise us by knocking over some penalties – a total of five in the game – but Bath came back with another try after Guscott chipped ahead and collected a kick-on from Adebayo to score under the posts. We were 25–18 behind and time was running out. I asked for an immense effort to see us through. We kept the pressure on by running a penalty. Bath were simply trying to stop us gaining any momentum, but we kept our drives going and managed to put King over on the short side for a try. I could not even watch the conversion and neither, I suspect, could most of the team, but Rees put that pressure kick over and we finished all square. So, from our four games with Leicester and Bath we had collected five points out of the eight available – an excellent return against such quality opposition. After eighteen games we had a three-point lead over Leicester, who had played sixteen games, and a six-point lead over Bath who had played seventeen games.

Wasps 25 Bath 25

Wasps	*Bath*
G Rees	M Perry
S Roiser	J Sleightholme
N Greenstock	P de Glanville
R Henderson	J Guscott
K Logan	A Adebayo
A King	M Catt
A Gomarsall	A Nichol
D Molloy	K Yates
S Mitchell	F Mendez
W Green	J Mallett
M Greenwood	G Llanes
A Reed	M Haag
L Dallaglio	N Thomas
M White	R Webster
C Sheasby	D Lyle

Scorers
Wasps. Try: King. Penalties: Rees (5). Conversion: Rees. Dropped goal: King.
Bath. Tries: Guscott (2), Adebayo. Penalties: Catt (2). Conversions: Callard, Catt.

Replacements
Wasps: S Mitchell replaced by K Dunn (53), W Green replaced by I Dunston (75), C Sheasby replaced by P Scrivener (65).
Bath: M Perry replaced by J Callard (75), A Nichol replaced by C Harrison (66).

The following Tuesday night I turned on the teletext as Alice and I were eating and saw that Leicester were leading

Gloucester at half time 19–9. I didn't expect Leicester to loose, they would probably go on to have a hard-earned victory at Kingsholm. I didn't bother looking at the TV again until my physio phoned up. As I was enjoying a bottle of red wine over dinner, he said, 'You'll never guess what, Gloucester have beaten Leicester 33–32.' I thought he was having me on – I turned on the teletext, and when I saw that it was true I was absolutely delighted. That was the turning point for me because up until then it had been beyond our control, but now the balance of power had shifted. If we won our remaining three games, no one could catch us. That was a very nice feeling indeed. We now had a chance to pull away from the pack and that gave us the extra desire we needed for the game against Saracens.

12 APRIL 1997

Courage League Division One: Saracens 15 Wasps 28

We had been to Saracens in the cup and lost but now we felt very determined; we knew what our options were, and our defensive operation was proving itself match by match. We felt that aggressive defence was going to be very important at this stage. Saracens were missing Michael Lynagh but everyone else who mattered was there so we had to keep them pinned down. We scored a pushover try, which is always reassuring, and Logan scored twice.

Saracens 15 Wasps 28

Saracens	*Wasps*
M Singer	G Rees
M Ebongalame	S Roiser
P Sella	N Greenstock
S Ravenscroft	R Henderson
R Wallace	K Logan
A Lee	A King
K Bracken	A Gomarsall
T Daly	D Molloy
G Botterman	S Mitchell

A Olver	W Green
P Johns	M Greenwood
T Copsey	A Reed
F Pienaar	L Dallaglio
R Hill	M White
A Diprose	C Sheasby

Scorers
Saracens. Tries: Botterman, Diprose. Penalty: Lee. Conversion: Lee.
Wasps: Tries: Logan (2), Sheasby. Penalties: Rees (3). Conversions: Rees (2).

Replacements
Saracens: P Johns replaced by C Yandell (74 minutes).
Wasps: S Mitchell replaced by K Dunn (71), M Greenwood replaced by D Cronin (71).

19 APRIL 1997

Courage League Division One: Wasps 36 Sale 10

The feeling in training was now fantastic; we knew that we had a very good chance of winning the championship indeed. It was the last home game of the season and a chance for us to finish off the season in style, in front of our crowd. It was the last home game for Bill Threadwell, club president for the last three years. He has done an outstanding job for us and I don't think we let him or anyone else down. We put in a really big performance. We defended superbly and we made a huge amount of tackles.

I think people thought the game was going to be a lot closer than it was. We owed Sale respect but they were obviously disrupted by injuries. If they put their best fifteen players on the pitch they can be a real handful and capable of beating any side. It was also to our advantage they had their eyes on the Pilkington Cup Final. We really hit them with a very physical, disciplined and professional performance and came off the pitch feeling extremely happy with the way we had played.

We were now the clear leaders. Bath were the only team that could catch us.

Wasps 36 Sale 10

Wasps	*Sale*
G Rees	J Mallinder
S Roiser	D Rees
N Greenstock	A Hadley
R Henderson	J Baxendell
K Logan	T Beim
A King	S Mannix
M Wood	D Morris
D Molloy	P Winstanley
S Mitchell	S Diamond
W Green	A Smith
M Greenwood	D Baldwin
A Reed	D Erskine
L Dallaglio	J Mitchell
M White	D O'Grady
C Sheasby	C Vyvyan

Scorers
Wasps. Tries: Henderson, Logan, Roiser, Greenstock. Penalties: Rees (3). Conversions: Rees (2). Dropped goal: King.
Sale. Try: Beim. Penalty: Mannix. Conversion: Hadley.

Replacements
Wasps: A Reed replaced by D Cronin (72 minutes), M White replaced by P Scrivener (53).
Sale: S Mannix replaced by C Yates (17).

26 APRIL 1997

Courage League Division One:
Northampton 15 Wasps 26

Having just beaten Sale, we knew that we needed to secure one more win from the remaining two games in order to become champions. But those two games were both against very strong opposition, Northampton and Harlequins, and both were away from home. However, we had a clear objective, and the title that we had fought so hard for all season was going to be ours. The press were already suggesting that the title race was over, that it was a foregone conclusion, which is always fatal. They were saying that Wasps were virtually there, that we'd as good as won the league – I think that not only caused problems in our own camp but also gave Northampton a bit of a spur. So we had two enemies to face – the press and Northampton – but it was crucial that we tried to focus as much as possible on the latter, a team we knew we could beat as we had beaten them earlier in the season. There was, however, no doubt that they were going to give us a tough game.

Our record against Northampton has never really been that brilliant, particularly at Franklin's Gardens where, out of our last ten visits, I think we've only won once or twice. Northampton's form had been particularly good this season and they'd only lost twice at home, once to Harlequins in the league and once to Sale in the Pilkington Cup. They had beaten Bath and Leicester at home, so clearly it wasn't going to be an easy match. Given the circumstances, the build-up to this game was different to that of a normal game and we were trying to stay as low-profile as possible.

Those pundits who thought that the result was a foregone conclusion, that this was to be an easier-than-normal task for Wasps, may have taken account of the fact that Northampton had some injury problems: Rodber was unlikely to start the game, Grayson was already sidelined with a hip injury and the young and relatively inexperienced Hepher had been brought in to the side – they were clearly operating at less than full strength. However, what we tried to do was no different to normal and something that had proved successful in the past: to look at the opposition, to look at ourselves, to pinpoint exactly how we were going to beat them – and then just hope that things would go our way. The performance against Sale at home had been a really solid encounter in which we had outplayed them in all areas of the game, and we had defended superbly, so I was just a little bit worried, going into the Northampton game, about how many playing minutes we had left in us. Had we enough gas in the tank to play out the last two games or, more importantly, to win this next game and hence the league? There's always that danger of peaking too soon and I just felt a little worried that perhaps we weren't going to play as well again.

Everyone was incredibly excited about the prospect of being able to wrap up the league with one game to go. To win the Courage League is an achievement, but to do it with a game to spare is an even greater one. I think we had been very fortunate throughout the season with injuries and we had kept ourselves fit, but I think people were now realising that if we were going to do it then it had to be this game – we didn't want to leave it to the last game of the season, particularly away from home against our arch rivals Harlequins. Players were starting to feel tired and the season was taking its toll.

We travelled to Northampton on the Saturday morning; anything else might have upset the players' natural routines and made them feel under even more pressure to get a result. The weather wasn't perhaps what either side wanted – it was a constant drizzle, bound to make the game even closer. Northampton always have very noisy support; they're not nasty people but they certainly make their presence felt with their rattles and brass bands. Matt Dawson was captain for the day, probably quite an inspired choice by Ian McGeechan. Matt had endured an indifferent season, spending a long time on the sidelines with injury, but here was a chance to come back and captain Northampton. He knew, and I'm sure the rest of his team knew, that the entire press core would be there, as would various dignitaries from the RFU and Sky TV. I think that probably gave them the inspiration they needed to think that they could win the game. Also, Northampton had given us a good battle at Loftus Road in a game which they probably thought they deserved to win. So I don't think Northampton feared anything from us.

It was very noisy beforehand, something that a lot of players in that changing room had never really experienced before. We were now on the verge of winning the hardest competition in domestic rugby and there were a lot of nerves, probably more so than if we had been playing at home, but that's understandable. However, at the same time, there was also a sense of total confidence, a feeling that everyone would give their all and that no one was prepared to take a backward step. The atmosphere of sheer determination and team spirit would, I felt sure, be enough to win the game.

To come off such a good performance against Sale and then to try and maintain that standard was always going to be difficult but that was our game plan. We were very proud of our defence but had no intention of relying on it – when we had the ball we would turn the tables and put pressure on them by keeping possession for long periods of play. We knew it was going to be a close game so it was vital that we nailed them as and when they came.

The game couldn't have got off to a worse start for us: they kicked off, won the ball and put us under pressure for the first 25 minutes. Their forwards were picking and driving and really had the bit between their teeth. The crowd was getting right behind them. Matt Dawson was just popping, and making the odd little break himself, and we were really under the cosh. But, as in previous games, we were able to absorb the pressure, and that's something we became very good at towards the end of the season. Northampton got a couple of penalties and went 6–0 up and we had hardly touched the ball. I think that's when you have to dig deep and believe in yourselves, believe that you can just absorb the pressure and weather the storm. Fortunately, we had a couple of attacks up field and we got back on level terms. Gareth Rees kicked a couple of penalties and Northampton responded again. I think it was then that we realised that this was going to be an eighty-minute game; they weren't just going to lay down and let us have the championship. Towards the end of the first half, we created one of the game's few opportunities: Gareth was instrumental in the move – he threw a lovely miss-pass to Shane Roiser who used his pace, took his chance and scored on the outside. Gareth came up trumps with the kick from the touchline, from his wrong side, which is something that he'd done all season. It gave us the lift that we needed, and at a crucial time.

We were relieved to be in front at half time. We'd been under pressure for the majority of the first half, but we'd taken our chances and gone ahead. Unfortunately, we were only ahead by a few points and it was clear that it was going to take a monumental effort to maintain the lead because Northampton were scenting a famous victory. It was going to be a very difficult second half indeed. Again, mine and Rob Smith's half-time team talk centred on the team remaining patient and disciplined, not to concede as much possession as we had done so far. It had seemed as though every time we got the ball we gave it away whereas whenever they got the ball they seemed to keep it and put us under enormous pressure. We all agreed that we were going to have to tackle our hearts out in this half, and with a huge effort the league title would be ours.

I wouldn't say that everything I'd asked for had gone in one ear and out of the other, but when we started the second half Northampton immediately dominated play and controlled possession yet again. They are very good at retaining possession. However, they didn't recognise that you've got to go forward at the same time and so we were able to shadow them across the field. Perhaps they were a little bit over-ambitious but every time they spread the ball we seemed to have an extra black shirt there to tackle them. Maybe we were firing on high octane at that stage of the season – we had everything to play for and they had nothing. One thing I've tried to ensure at Wasps is that when the guys make a tackle they don't try and chase lost causes and get their hands all over the ball and kill it, that they just get up and make another one. I think that always gave us the extra man over, and in this particular game it paid huge dividends. But they still put us under an enormous amount of pressure: Dawson played very well; Martin Bayfield was having a super game having just returned from injury; their fly half, Hepher, was looking very assured for his age and Thorneycroft and Hunter were making pretty decisive runs from the back. It was touch and go at one stage and they had a number of scrums on or in our 22. But we took our chances and they didn't. They had a number of opportunities in the second half where they put us under pressure but failed to score, and we managed to limit them to kicks at goal.

When we entered the last ten minutes of the game you could sense that we were growing in confidence. We seemed to repel any attack that they threw at us, and they threw everything they had. It was a huge team effort. The coaches were aware of how physically demanding the game had been. I think Wasps had been very sensible with the way they'd used tactical substitutions throughout the season and this game proved to be no exception. They took Andy Reed off – after he and Matt Greenwood had made an incredible try-saving double-tackle together – and brought Damian Cronin on, just to give the team that bit of a lift through having some fresh legs. With about five minutes to go we had a scrum just outside our own 22. We were very street-wise and did something which is probably not common in the Wasps rugby handbook: we had about four or five consecutive scrums and we just held the ball at the back, driving them back and wheeling it round – well within the laws of the game – just to run the clock down.

Eventually we broke from a back-row move from the base of the scrum and Gareth Rees, who had moved to fly half at this stage because of an injury to Alex King, put the ball right down in the corner and you could feel that we only had to hold out for a couple of minutes longer and the league would be ours. Northampton were still in the game but then Gareth managed to scoop a knock-on off the floor and passed it to Kenny Logan who went in under the posts. Kenny has an eye for a try – he had scored eleven in nine games up to that point – and we knew then, as did everyone else, that the title was ours.

When the final whistle went, it was a very emotional moment for everyone. We came together in a huddle and felt justifiably very proud of each other. Everyone who was involved with the team came on the pitch to join us. It had been a huge squad effort, all season long, and I think everyone recognised the role that everyone else had played. They were obviously very emotional moments for everyone concerned.

At the time, there had only been three names on the league trophy – Bath, Leicester and ourselves – and to win it in the manner that we had done that time round was especially gratifying. No one could take that away from us – we had done it with a game to spare, and the sense of achievement at that particular moment was just fantastic. We were presented with the trophy by the President of the RFU, John Richardson. A number of former Wasps captains had come to the game as well – Roger Uttley, Mark Rigby, Sir Peter Yarrenton – so it was a particularly emotional time for them, too.

I'm used to doing team talks in the dressing room after games and it's usually, 'Let's not get carried away, there are plenty of games left.' It's either that or something of a verbal blast, but on this occasion it was just a very noisy celebration. We all got together in the changing rooms for a team photo – even Mark Rigby got himself in the changing room, I don't quite know how, and he was celebrating with us as well – it was fantastic.

We've always had good times at Northampton, although this is a part of the sport which is now diminishing slowly as the game becomes more and more professional and teams fly in and out. But on this occasion, we had the time to indulge our urge to celebrate; we were able to stay up there for a couple of hours and enjoyed a victory drink with our supporters, a good many of whom travelled up for the game. The one thing I noticed was the number of people who came to the game from London – a huge travelling contingent and probably more than I've ever seen during my involvement with the club.

We hadn't planned anything in case things went horribly wrong so it was a spontaneous celebration; we decided to head back to the club first and then go from there. Obviously, the coach trip was one huge party, as it would be with any team which had just won the league. We certainly had a few drinks on the bus and a fantastic sing-song. When we got back to Sudbury we were greeted with scenes we didn't expect. There must have been three or four thousand people there and we had to walk through a wall of supporters to get to the clubhouse. The party that we were about to witness went on to the early hours of the morning. The club decided that it was time to lift the tariff on the bar, and a good time was had by everyone. Obviously, the supporters welcomed this, particularly after what has been for them a very difficult season in adapting to professionalism. Perhaps a lot of them felt that they had been pushed away from the players. It's always been a factor at Wasps that the players and supporters have been able to mingle, maybe more so than at other clubs, and I think that, with the teething problems at Loftus Road, this was something that had perhaps been denied them this season. So when we turned up at Sudbury it was a nice touch for them. They were obviously very happy that we'd won but they were also very happy that we'd come back to share that success with them – and they gave us a heroes' welcome.

Northampton 15 Wasps 26

Northampton	*Wasps*
I Hunter	G Rees
N Beal	S Roiser
G Townsend	N Greenstock
M Allen	R Henderson
H Thorneycroft	K Logan

A Hepher	A King
M Dawson	M Wood
M Volland	D Molloy
A Clarke	S Mitchell
M Stewart	W Green
J Phillips	M Greenwood
M Bayfield	A Reed
S Foale	L Dallaglio
J Cassell	M White
D Merlin	C Sheasby

Scorers
Northampton. Penalties: Hepher (5).
Wasps. Tries: Roiser, Logan. Penalties: Rees (4). Conversions: Rees (2).

Replacements
Northampton: G Townsend replaced by C Moir (25 minutes).
Wasps: A King replaced by J Ufton (78), A Reed replaced by D Cronin (61), M White replaced by P Scrivener (79).

3 MAY 1997

Courage League Division One: Harlequins 22 Wasps 42

The chance of playing at Harlequins, of going there as league champions, and with a team that wanted to play for each other, was too good to miss, and I think everyone made themselves available for selection. There was a normal Monday meeting after the Northampton game and I can honestly say that, despite some phenomenal celebrations that had taken place over the weekend, everyone was sober by the time they reported in for work on that morning. Over the 21 league games that we had played to date, Harlequins were the only team that had beaten us at home. We could think of nothing better than going there as defending champions and setting the record straight. All credit to Harlequins, they deserved to be the only side that had beaten us at home, but it was important that we signed off as champions.

When we were given the shirts for the game the club had already had printed on them '1996–97 Courage League

Champions', which was, I think, the only touch of arrogance that we displayed for the entire day. We didn't start the game particularly well; although we scored an early try they came back at us and at half time it was still anyone's game. But in the second half we really stepped things up. To be fair to Harlequins, they were without certain key players, which had obviously affected their game plan. They were missing Gary Connolly and Will Carling, who had been in great form, but we really played well and everyone in the team seemed to be getting in on the party. Rob Henderson had a particularly good game, and in the end it turned out to be a very comprehensive victory.

To score forty points against any side is a fair achievement. To score it against a side very close to the top of the league themselves is even better. We had beaten one of the best teams in the country comprehensively and at home – that gave us a tremendous amount of satisfaction. We were delighted to have won the league by as big a margin as six points. It had been billed as the most competitive league ever, and the hardest ever season, and it had taken some doing to win it, but we had won it in style. Our support base, which seemed to be growing all the time, sent a tremendous contingent to Harlequins and they were rewarded with our lap of honour with the trophy.

Harlequins 22 Wasps 42

Harlequins	*Wasps*
J Staples	J Ufton
D O'Leary	S Roiser
J Keyter	N Greenstock
T Lacroix	R Henderson
M Corcoran	K Logan
P Challinor	G Rees
R Sharples	A Gomarsall
L Benezech	D Molloy
T Billups	S Mitchell
J Leonard	W Green
G Llewellyn	M Greenwood

L Gross	A Reed
G Allison	L Dallaglio
L Cabannes	M White
B Davison	C Sheasby

Scorers

Harlequins. Tries: Allison, Cabannes, Keyter. Penalty: Lacroix. Conversions: Lacroix, Corcoran.

Wasps. Tries: Logan (2), Henderson (2), Green, Rees. Penalties: Rees (2). Conversions: Rees (3).

Replacements

Harlequins: T Lacroix replaced by R Dables (52 minutes), L Benezech replaced by A Mullins (71), G Allison replaced by P Delaney (75), B Davison replaced by S Owen (56).

Wasps: S Mitchell replaced by K Dunn (66), M White replaced by D Cronin (68), C Sheasby replaced by P Scrivener (57).

As we had secured the title away from home, a lot of our supporters had missed out on celebrating the championship success with us. Naturally, we wanted to get everyone – the first team, the second team, the development team, the management team, the fitness team, the back-up staff and those involved in the business side of things – together under one roof and celebrate the input from everyone and the fact that their input had culminated in a tremendous achievement. The party was held in the Rose Room at Twickenham, which has the ideal facilities and surroundings to cater for such a celebration. It wasn't too formal and we enjoyed a great dinner which Chris Wright generously financed. I had to get up and make an impromptu speech; but given the occasion and the emotion involved it didn't matter that I was unprepared. I thanked Chris Wright and everyone else involved for giving us the opportunity, giving us that extra edge we needed to push for the title, something which we had lacked in previous seasons. And, once things wound down, the party continued into the early hours of the morning in true Wasps fashion.

I had thought that in this first professional season of English rugby, the team that was going to win the championship wouldn't necessarily be the team with the highest payroll, the team with the foreign superstars or the team with the best facilities or the greatest resources. It would be the team that were the most professional and I think that, all round, we reflected that – we became the most professional team in the country. I'm sure that other teams will adapt during the 1997–98 season so we will have to find new ways to remain one step ahead.

A lot of people suggested that the championship was won by our defence. However, Wasps averaged over 31 points per game, and that's clearly not a side which just defends. We felt we had an all-round game and I believe there are a number of reasons why we triumphed. One of them I would attribute to Pat Fox, the guy in charge of fitness at Wasps, as I would say we were fitter than any other side in the league. We had very few muscular injuries – general conditioning injuries which keep players out for one or two weeks – and that was down to Pat Fox. We were also lucky in that we didn't have any major injuries and Damian Hopley was really the only player unavailable for selection for a long time. We had a professional expertise that cannot be found anywhere else in the country – anything that the players needed was available to them. A player could turn up on the Monday morning, after a hard league game, carrying an injury which should normally take three weeks to put right, but he would be match-fit for the following Saturday. Obviously, in order to do this a club needs the right environment and professional medical expertise – and Wasps have it all.

Wasps' director of rugby, Nigel Melville, was another influential figure. He bought and sold players sensibly and managed the day-to-day affairs of the club to great effect. He was always available to talk to which was very important when many players felt uncertain about their futures. Again, Rob Smith found his true role in the team as head coach; he was obviously very confident in what Nigel was doing and was therefore able to concentrate wholly on his task – and he did that superbly well. Basically, the team comprising Nigel Melville, Rob Smith, Roger Uttley, John Lamden and Pat Fox had displayed an infectious enthusiasm for the club and for the competition, and that is something you need in a very long and arduous season with all its highs and lows. They had an ability to inspire the team at any given moment, which again is something very difficult to do. I think that our success is not just a testament to the individual players involved but a testimony to the Wasps family. I think that sums it up better than anything.

There was a definite turning point in the season: we lost heavily to Munster and then, within a week, we thrashed Toulouse, scoring 77 points. I think that tells you something. If you lose three games and then give the European champions a sound beating, you turn the club round. We certainly had it in us to perform to that level, but whatever we were doing beforehand was clearly not working. We'd had some very good league wins, but that particular week turned the whole season round for us, and that particular game was the best I've ever been involved in as a Wasps player.

In any campaign there are defining moments, and the last-minute kick against Bristol by Alex King was clearly one – he won the game from the touchline in injury time. That match against Toulouse and another last-minute try by Alex King, this time against Bath, were also vital. One of the most memorable games was the one up at Leicester. We left Welford Road with a lot more confidence and in much better health than when we arrived and, although Leicester won the game, that was the turning point in their season. After that game they went downhill and we took confidence from the game. I remember saying afterwards that we would go on and win the league.

We had vastly experienced players but probably the key player within the whole set-up was Gareth Rees, the eternal journeyman who had come home to Wasps. He had played at Wasps as a youngster, and in the John Player Cup Final, and had then gone on to various clubs before rejoining us. He was someone who really performed incredibly well and when we signed him we knew exactly what we were getting. He'd finished the previous season three points behind Neil Jenkins in the all-time Welsh leagues in terms of point scoring. He'd finished on 293 points, a phenomenal achievement when you consider that he hadn't played in every league game. To be successful in rugby you need a goal kicker, you need a points machine, and we had one in Gareth Rees – he carried us through a lot of games and was of paramount importance to our title ambitions. But it wasn't just his goal kicking. It was also his experience – he's captained Canada and he's played in a vast number of internationals – that was vital to us.

Other key players would have to include Matthew Greenwood, Richard Kinsey, Buster White and Kevin Dunn, those kind of experienced players who played a very important role – perhaps because they had been involved in a number of Wasp teams which had nearly won titles. In their first season, Matthew Greenwood and Kevin Dunn had finished runners-up in the league to Bath. Now they wanted to finish their careers at Wasps with something to show for it. That kind of experience, and that kind of attitude, is crucial. I mean, every club would want to have players like Matt Greenwood and Buster White in their team, there's no doubt about that. In my view, Buster White was very unfortunate not to go on the Argentina tour with England.

9 The Lions Tour

The assembly point for the 1997 British Lions tour came fast. Saying goodbye to Alice and Ella was difficult. Ella was six weeks old and when I next saw her she would be eight weeks older. It was very difficult to get to grips with this, so we kept our goodbyes very short and sweet. Having never been involved in a Lions tour before, I discovered a tremendous amount of anticipation and expectation. To be selected for the Lions, and particularly to tour South Africa, the existing world champions, really is the pinnacle of anyone's rugby career. Having been there with England in 1994 and seen the facilities and witnessed the aura that rugby creates in South Africa, I looked upon this tour as a mouth-watering opportunity.

I took a taxi over to Jason Leonard's house, jumped in his car with him and we picked up Keith Wood on the way down to Weybridge. That's when I really got the feeling that I was now in a different team altogether: two Englishmen picking up an Irishman and then heading to the team's headquarters – I sensed that this was going to be something very special. I kept asking Jason questions, kept badgering him, kept pestering him about what it was going to be like: What should I pack? Would they give me enough clothes? What would I need? I just leaned on his experience – he had been involved in the Lions tour of New Zealand in 1993 and I wanted to get an idea from him about what to expect. I had that sense of going into the unknown and I wanted to know what was going on.

When we arrived at the Oaklands Park Hotel we walked into the reception area and were greeted with all the faces that I'd been reading about over the last couple of weeks. It was probably easier for an Englishman to turn up as there were eighteen of us selected for the tour – so you were saying hello to all your old friends, familiar faces, guys who you had played with or against in the last few weeks. Being an Irishman, Welshman or a Scotsman must have been a lot more difficult because there were not as many of them. However, the fact that there are now a fair number of Welsh, Irish and Scottish players involved in the English domestic leagues must have made it easier for them. The multinational composition of the squad was hammered home to us all during that particular meeting.

Everyone was wondering why we were having a pre-tour week together, something very different to any other tour I'd been on. Wasn't it bad enough that we were away for seven weeks without having an extra week in Weybridge? I think everyone was a little bit miffed and slightly puzzled over what we would be doing during this week. The rumour had spread that there wasn't going to be much rugby training, so what was going to happen? We'd already met as a preliminary British Lions squad a few weeks before, again something which had never been done in the past but, for me, it indicated how professional the 1997 Lions were going to be. The management had started thinking about this tour a long time ago. Fran Cotton, Ian McGeechan and Jim Telfer had planned this methodically and thoroughly, and they'd even involved a number of players who could not be in the final 35. They wanted to let everyone know as much as possible and give everyone plenty of time to start reflecting on what it was going to take to go out there and win. I was struck by the professionalism of the whole set-up and this was obviously very encouraging to us all.

The squad would comprise 35 players and a 12-strong management back-up team, so we were a squad of 47. They emphasised that without the cooperation and the assistance of all 47 people the trip would not be successful. It was bewildering to see how much research had been done. For instance, Ian McGeechan, the head coach, had spent a number of weeks with John Hart, the New Zealand coach, because New Zealand had won their last series in South Africa. Ian had obviously been out there to gain ideas and pick up useful hints on how to make the 1997 Lions a successful team. The most important thing was the 35-player element; never before in the history of the Lions had they taken that many players on tour with them, and that was going to be the key factor. The other thing which I found important was that Andy Keast had come on board. He had been director of rugby for Natal when I was there with England in 1994 and he had been very successful – they won the Currie Cup twice – and obviously his understanding of South African rugby was far greater than anyone else's. We had our own masseur, a team doctor, a team physio and even a media liaison officer, an entirely new position. However, we were about to go on a professional tour and we were going to have over 200 media employees with us virtually every day, so we needed someone to coordinate relations. Also for the first time we had a 'lioness' looking after us; Sam Peters would help the manager and the liaison officer, Bob Burrows, to do their jobs. Everyone was brought on that tour for a specific role and that was made evident by Fran in his opening speech.

Another thing that struck me as being important was the fact that Fran and Ian had obviously had a tremendous amount of experience in touring South Africa themselves so they knew what it took to win there. Fran, a very successful businessman, a huge character and a very successful rugby player, had won a Test series in South Africa and so had Ian. These guys were able to pass their experience on to us. Fran emphasised that there were some key, core values that were going to have to be taken on board if we were to win. Desire was one of them – we knew that there were going to be testing times ahead and so we had to have the greatest desire to win because you could bet your bottom dollar that the South Africans would have all the desire that they needed – they could pack it in a bottle and sell it. Attitude was also going to be crucial. With a lot of players away on tour, not everyone was going to be happy at any one given time. The attitude in training, in pre-matches, during matches, post-match, over a long period of time was going to be tested to the limit. Discipline was another factor, not just on the pitch, but off it as well. This was the first professional Lions tour and there would be elements within the tour that hadn't existed previously. For instance, the amount of media coverage was probably going to be twice what it had been on any other tour. South Africa is an enjoyable country and it's one that, if you are not careful, can be over-enjoyed to the detriment of the rugby. Another thing was intelligence. The management team had already demonstrated a high degree of intelligence in the way that they had gone about their business and if we were to fulfil our potential as a playing squad then we were going to have to be an equally intelligent group of people.

Perhaps most important of all would be self-belief. When you play against South Africa you are not just playing against the team, you are playing against the entire nation, and we were told that the only people that were going to believe that we would win would be ourselves and probably our closest family. Everyone else had already written us off. A lot of people were saying that it was going to be 3–0 in the Test series. The majority of the press were suggesting that it had been a long and arduous campaign domestically and this would prove to be a tour too far; a test series that we were going to lose. We had to be a family from the moment we arrived at Weybridge to the moment we landed back in London.

For the week in Weybridge we were to do some training but primarily we would be involved with Impact, a team-building company from Cumbria. They were brought in to ensure that, when the 1997 Lions squad left the hotel on the Saturday, we were a team, that we had an identity, that we had values, that we had objectives, that we understood each other and that we were prepared to lay down and die for each other. The task was to be completed in just five days, so they had quite a big remit. It was no easy task. They introduced themselves and outlined what they planned to do with us for the rest of the week without giving away too many ideas. It was going to be an interesting week.

We then went back to our rooms. I was sharing with Eric Miller, whom I had never properly met before, other than on the pitch. I had played against him only once or twice up till then. The interesting thing was that, although there were eighteen Englishmen there, I was immediately put in a room with an Irishman. This deliberate and, I think, sensible policy of mingling the four nationalities was maintained throughout the tour. Rather than being placed in a familiar environment, a recognisable comfort zone, each player was forced to make an effort by being placed with an unfamiliar teammate. Eric is a super guy, and one of the finds of the season – a vastly talented runner and rugby player who I'm sure will go on to achieve great things. It was good to be with him and we got on famously.

We had been told, in no uncertain terms, to bring very little kit with us, but with everyone no doubt feeling a little bit panicky we all brought far too much. Then we were given our official Adidas kits and we immediately understood the previous instruction – we had now been given a huge amount. When you get your kit it gives you a real sense of identity, you see that famous crest, that famous badge – it's just incredible.

An element of the squad had previous Lions experience, but I hadn't, and Eric was the same. Eric had only played two seasons of rugby, so he was just as bewildered as I was. We spent a lot of time looking at the phenomenal amount of kit. We had training kit, we had casual wear, we had formal wear and we had informal wear. Again, being the professional outfit that the Lions were, they had catered for every eventuality – in fact, it's safe to say that they had over catered for every eventuality. We ended up taking stuff out there for which we had no use at all, but we had it just in case, that was the important thing. In case it was cold, for instance. We wanted to be the most professional, so we didn't want to risk getting out there and discovering Arctic conditions and us not having the right gear.

Once all those formalities were out of the way, we could get on with what was about to unfold with Impact, the team-building group. It was clear to see that, in the first instance, it was going to be back to the classroom, and that was something which I think a lot of the guys weren't overjoyed to discover. It is always dangerous when people outside rugby, and who perhaps haven't been involved in any major tour before, suddenly come in and start telling rugby players what they intend to do with them. They were not rugby players and I think they were a little bit wary of that fact, but at the same time they were obviously very confident in their approach to the task at hand. They had obviously been successful with a number of other organisations before; they had gone into businesses and sorted them out, so they were confident that they could do the same with us. What we eventually did was to embark on a series of exercises. We were split into groups, which were changed every other day, and we were given a series of challenges. It was a bit like being on *The Crystal Maze* really – a skill game, a mental game, a physical game – and there was a bit of fun to it as well.

Obviously we had a lot of guys who had never met each other before. I had never met David Young for instance, I didn't know Scott Gibbs, Keith Wood, Eric Miller, Jeremy Davidson or Alan Tait particularly well, so it was just a way of getting everyone to interact really. From the outset, it was obvious that, for things to work out for us, we would all have to be prepared to have an open and meaningful dialogue with one another. Impact set tasks that weren't easy, that couldn't be done in seconds or minutes; they had to be worked on as a team or they could not be completed. For instance, they had this contraption that looked like a spider's web: there were many different-sized holes and each member of the group had to pass through a different one, aided by the rest, without touching the sides. We couldn't just throw each other through. We had to decide as a team – and quickly – who was going to go through which hole, what technique we were to use and who would be doing the lifting.

Another challenge that encouraged interpersonal dialogue and activity was a crate-building exercise, the objective of which was to put as many crates on top of each other, and then one of the group would have to stand on the top, to prove that it was a proper structure. It wasn't just a question of putting crates up and one of you standing up there; the guy who was to stand up there was going to be suspended, so it involved two or three of the team supporting him with guide ropes from each side and someone else passing the crates up. That one in particular created a great deal of competition between the groups. Yet another exercise, just a straightforward one, involved climbing up a very thin rope ladder to the top of a particularly high oak tree – about 50 foot. A number of the group were scared of heights but, in the competitive group environment, they wanted to achieve and they didn't want to let the team down so they overcame their vertigo problems and went up like squirrels.

It was very interesting and we would go away and discuss what we felt was good and why we achieved it, why were we successful. If we weren't particularly good at an exercise we would discuss why things went wrong and how we could improve it if we were to do it again. The groups changed as well, so you weren't always working with the same people. To become interactive was exactly what we needed to do, it helped in team meetings and I felt sure that it would help us out when we faced problems and challenges on the field later on. The discovery, encouragement and nurture of team spirit within this positive and competitive team culture, was of tremendous benefit. It was clear that we now had a group of players who were beginning to get on very well indeed. Although I think the exercises were a tremendous success, they weren't accepted with open arms by every member of the tour party. Some people felt that the days were long – from eight in the morning to seven at night – and, recognising the rigours of a particularly hard season, thought that we just needed to rest. We were working very hard. But the management, and in particular Impact, felt that this was absolutely necessary; they only had five days to get the team together, and we were therefore going to have to work at that level of intensity. So it was difficult, but I think it was well worth it.

We were doing rugby training as well. We were using the London Irish training ground and it was there that I gained first-hand experience of Jim Telfer. A number of the players had worked with him in the past and so had some idea of what to expect but we suspected that he had been told not to do too much with us, not to flog us too early. Well, I remember thinking that if that wasn't too much then we should all be worried about what was to come. We did plenty of tackle bag work and plenty of running around. Again, it was important to get a feel for each other and really try to get the show on the road, to kick things off. And it was enjoyable. I think what came out of all that was the fact that we weren't going to have any short training sessions. Already we were training for about two hours per day and we hadn't set foot in South Africa yet. So I think it was pretty evident to us all that there was a tremendous amount of hard work ahead.

What the management wanted to happen was for us as players to create our own core values for the tour. This was our tour, and they wanted us to set the goalposts for the duration. So the last exercise of the week, and perhaps the most significant, was for us to establish what we felt was important to the tour, and to agree our own guidelines, the 1997 Lions Laws if you like. Again, we split up into groups to discuss the issues and then we came back and discussed them as a team. Obviously, there was a lot of overlap, several groups were thinking along the same lines, and from that we were able to establish some guidelines that were to carry us through the entire tour.

We decided there were to be financial fines from the players' court, which is itself a tradition. We wanted to have a tour that had some familiar aspects, and the players' court has always been a factor. There was a danger that because this was a professional tour the court would not happen but the players were pretty determined that it would. The important thing was to establish a disciplinary committee to deal with the offences which inevitably occur, on and off the pitch, on any tour. The players decided that the committee would be judge and jury on any serious disciplinary matters and it was formed with four people: Fran Cotton, Ian McGeechan, Rob Wainwright and Martin Johnson, the captain.

Another issue that was discussed concerned selection and polarisation. This was very important indeed. Non-selected players felt that they should congratulate players that were selected in their position. This was something that was probably hitherto unheard of. Individuals may have done it, in private, but now, on this tour, selected players were also to publicly recognise the role of non-players. Furthermore, we decided that any selection queries should be taken to the coach and not discussed with other players. If you discuss that sort of thing with other players it can create disharmony and break the party. If we were going to win in South Africa we were going to have to be united at all times. We couldn't afford to show any cracks, any chinks in the armour, and that was something which was obviously vital. So, before the Tests, and on a purely confidential basis, non-selected players would be forewarned by the management so they wouldn't have, or show, as much disappointment when the team was officially announced. Letters were to be put under everyone's door the night before a Test match, to congratulate or commiserate. This was as a result of bitter lessons learned by some of the other players on previous tours, when they had expected to be selected but had been ruled out on borderline decisions – and they had found out only at the point of the official team announcement.

We also decided that focus was to be retained by all 35 players, before, during and after every game, and perhaps especially before the final two midweek games. What we didn't want was for the guys who had just played on a Saturday to automatically think that they should go off tour, and if the players who were playing in the midweek games were going to win then they would need the focus and support of every single member involved. So that brought us on to another issue, to make a concerted effort to get to know all members of the party. It seems obvious but, without making an effort, it is possible to go through a whole training session, even a whole week, without talking to certain individuals. I think one of the most important things here was to make the team room the focus of the party, not the bedroom. There was a team room in every port of call we had, including Weybridge. We would get all the social events and activities going there and we wouldn't break up into little splinter groups. The other thing was to have a daily meal together. You're eating so regularly as a rugby player that you tend to sit with certain people, you tend to go off with certain people, so we decided it was important to have one meal as a squad.

One more resolution was to organise an entertainments committee, to organise non-rugby related activities. The rugby was going to be so intense that it was clear we would need some diversions. And we thrived on these diversions. From the games we had played with Impact it was clear that these sorts of activity went down very well with the squad. In the end, John Bentley headed the entertainments committee – no surprise there. And he was in charge of picking his own team. He picked Jerry Guscott, I think purely from the point of view that if he didn't then Jerry would just ridicule anything that he suggested.

Another issue was communication. We felt that we needed weekly squad meetings, which wouldn't include the management, so we could kick a few things around. This was all about objective feedback. If the management had an issue with a player, they would go directly to the player concerned. We set up a senior player committee, or panel, to which any player in the squad could voice a concern. They might feel a little bit intimidated to voice that concern directly to the management, but they wouldn't to a player – they could remain anonymous. I was involved in that along with Martin Johnson, Scott Gibbs, Alan Tait and Paul Wallace. There was a common theme emerging here – any panel or form of player representation was made up of one player from each country plus the skipper.

The handling of the press was another issue which needed to be resolved. It was clear to every player that it was going to be a bit different to anything they had previously experienced and, rather than having the same players exposed all the time, we wanted to give everyone a chance to meet the press. So it was decided that Bob Burrows, the liaison officer, and Martin Johnson would nominate players for individual press conferences. The press perhaps might not always get the man they wanted, but it would be well managed.

Team spirit was, of course the most important aspect of the tour. It is the backbone of any side and it keeps people together. Basically what we were trying to do, particularly in training, was to motivate each other, to drive up the standards and stop any complacency creeping in.

Now, getting down to the nitty gritty, another important core value was the code of conduct. We created these laws, but they weren't cast in stone. They were merely guidelines that we had discussed as a team and felt that we should adhere to but if players decided to exclude themselves from those laws, then that was their choice. However, in the end, no one ever did. The code of conduct stated that no one was to go out to a party, or out drinking, or anything like that on pre-match nights. Alcohol had been a big issue on previous tours. But we decided it was an individual responsibility. If players wanted to drink then they could do so – as long as it was not detrimental to their own performance or to that of the team, which was paramount.

Punctuality and communication were also discussed. It was felt that the players should have some input into the tour's itinerary. During the tour, players wouldn't always be in the same team, so in order to remain punctual – to ensure that we would be in the right place at the right time – we needed to know exactly what was going on. Communication has to be a two-way process; otherwise all-important timing may be sacrificed. It would, however, be the duty of every player to find out where he needed to be and at what time.

We were instructed by the coaching staff on what we had to wear. This would ensure that the identity of the squad was maintained throughout the tour. We were also very aware that we had a duty to our sponsors, more so than on any previous tour, and that without them there would be no tour.

All of these things were discussed and decided during the final meeting with Impact. These were important issues which we had to take on board, issues and resolutions that had to last right the way through the whole South African tour. We obviously wouldn't have time to eradicate any problems arising out of any disagreements on tour and so the management, and Impact, had ensured that all such potential problem areas had been resolved before we set off. Every single member of that squad had had an input into, and an impact on, those laws. We were all agreed.

Everyone had responded to the call. When we arrived at the hotel on the Monday we were a bunch of individual players from different countries, yet when we boarded the coach for Heathrow just a few days later we were the British Lions, a team with an identity, a purpose, an objective and a collective spirit. All credit to Fran Cotton's management team and Impact.

We travelled in blazers – again something which wasn't argued over. That was something which had been basically decided in the code of conduct. You do as you're told. We travelled in blazers because of the amount of coverage the departure was going to receive; it was important that we looked smart, that we left Weybridge with the right message and that we sent out the right message to the South Africans – we were a team, we were united and we were ready for them. And as soon as we boarded the Virgin aircraft, we changed into tracksuits. I don't think the staff on board had seen anything like it: 35 guys who, as soon as they walked in the door, were off with their blazers and on with their tracksuits. We left united.

To be honest, I'd been thinking about South Africa ever since I had left there in 1994. I was very keen to go back. I'd won my first cap against South Africa and I felt that I would thrive on the challenge that they presented. I'd come on since then. We had lost that game as an England team but the 15 minutes that I played had given me a taste for it, and I wanted more. Other than that game, all my rugby had been played against northern hemisphere opposition, so it was a real chance for me personally. Cotton had said that, in his opinion, there was no better place to play rugby than the South African arena. Having been there in 1994, I had to agree with him. A lot of the players had been there in 1995, for the World Cup, and they had also witnessed something very special. It was incredible to think that we were going back. The thought was difficult to take on board, perhaps because we were surrounded with such luxury by Virgin. A lot of guys felt we were being wrapped in cotton wool, but certainly it made the trip a much easier one.

We flew from Heathrow to Johannesburg and the first thing that had to be done was the press conference where we were re-introduced to some familiar faces including Louis Luyt, president of SARFU. Louis, Martin Johnson,

Fran Cotton and Ian McGeechan took the top table and we were put at the sides. Louis expressed his delight at having the British Lions back in South Africa and then there was a chance for the South African media to put the usual questions to the British Lions management. It probably dragged on longer than the players wanted it to, but I think it really made everyone realise that we had actually arrived. Of course South Africa were talking up their rugby, but there was one common theme throughout the press conference, and Louis Luyt kept touching on this – they were all absolutely delighted that the British Lions were coming out to South Africa. It had been seventeen years since the last Lions tour, and the ghosts of 1974 had still not been put to bed.

Fran, Ian and Martin were obviously playing things down somewhat. There's a time and a place to throw down the gauntlet, and that was neither the time nor the place. So we swiftly flew on to Durban, one of the nicest places in South Africa and somewhere for which I have a great deal of affection.

There was a typical Zulu welcome, with dancers outside the Beverley Hills Hotel, north of the city. It really was roll-out-the-red-carpet stuff. The hotel was fairly luxurious by any tour standards – we had rooms looking out over the rocks on to the Indian Ocean. I was sharing with Rob Wainwright, which was an interesting mix because the two of us were obviously going to be fighting it out for the No. 6 spot in the Test team. However, I'd already known him for a number of years so, instead of being at each other's throats, we got on very well together.

Everything was so meticulously laid out. Every night we had a bit of paper put under the door, the itinerary for the next day. It consisted of what we were doing, which dress code was required, which colour training shirt, what time lunch was and any additional information we might need to know. So, from the word go, it was clear that the management were pretty determined that things were going to work like clockwork. There were so many things to be done, so many people had to be in different places at different times, that this was the only real way that things could be managed. It was obvious that Fran was going to run things with military precision.

So, on the first day we were at Kings Park, training. Ian McGeechan had been developing a playing style, which was still in its embryonic stages, and which he had been trying to put across to us at Weybridge. Now, we had to take that on a stage further but not get too carried away with ourselves. We had so much to achieve and in such a short space of time that I think there was a danger of over-complicating things too early in the tour. Day one was, therefore, really just an extension of what we had been doing, just to get the ball into people's hands, to get people feeling comfortable with each other and to work on a bit of rucking and a bit of continuity.

It was very hot in Durban, probably what we would call a hot summer's day, although it was the middle of their winter. It was somewhere between 80 and 90 degrees, so there was that to contend with as well.

The team was announced on Thursday when we left Durban. It's always pleasing to be selected for the first game. We'd now been training for a few days – everyone was really enthusiastic – and I think it was a huge relief for those selected, it certainly was for me. However, for those who weren't selected, it was obviously a huge disappointment – everyone was so enthusiastic about playing.

24 MAY 1997

Eastern Province XV 9 British Lions 41

The opening game was against my last opponents in South Africa. I remember that being a none-too-pretty game in which Tim Rodber was sent off, Jon Callard had twenty stitches in his head and I suffered numerous lacerations across the back – but we had won the game. Since then, I felt that I had grown up a lot in rugby terms, and now I was back at the scene of the crime, as it were, a much older and, I felt, a much wiser rugby player, and well able to handle myself. I was hoping and praying I would get picked for this first game so I could help set the record straight, not in any violent or malicious way, but just in pure rugby terms. Just to go out there and do the business.

The team meal was organised for the Thursday, prior to leaving for Port Elizabeth. We went to a restaurant called Langoustines, in Durban, a seafood restaurant which all the players thoroughly enjoyed. It provided a chance to get everyone together just before the tour really kicked off.

Port Elizabeth was slightly different to Durban in that we'd lost the sun and it was very overcast and damp. But it was now down to the serious business. It was important that the 1997 Lions got off to a flying start and threw down the gauntlet to the South Africans. For those fortunate enough to be selected for the first game, it was important that we really sent a positive message to those both outside and inside the squad. It was a fairly well balanced team, I thought. I hadn't played with Scott Quinnell before – the last time I had played against him he had scored four tries for Wales Youth against England Colts, so it was nice to be on the same team as him for once. Rob Howley, whom I had admired as a player during the Five Nations', was also selected and Jason Leonard was captain.

Eastern Province were a side that no one liked playing. They had been coached by Grizz Wyllie in 1994, the ex-All Black coach. They were a no-nonsense, fearsome outfit. But they were still in the doldrums of South African provincial rugby. However, when we arrived in 1997 there was clearly an upbeat feeling around Erasmus Park, or Telcom Park as they now call it, which is their home. They'd recently signed some high-standard players, including Theo van Rensburg who had been full back for Transvaal, and they also had some exciting young players coming through. Generally, there was a feeling that Eastern Province were on their way up. And, obviously, for them to entertain the Lions in their opening match was a tremendous honour for them. It was a sign that their status in the game was clearly improving. Kobus Wiese and Hennie le Roux, great servants of the green jersey for South Africa, and stars of the 1995 World Cup triumph over the All Blacks, were in the side, so they certainly weren't going to be a pushover. I was the last person who needed to be told it wasn't going to be an easy game.

The pre-match preparation went very well. We were now in a situation where we had been together for two weeks, we'd been training very hard, and we now needed to uncork the bottle, to get out on the pitch and start letting out a bit of the aggression which had been building up in training. It was certainly time to start playing. A lot of the guys, including myself, hadn't kicked a ball competitively for five weeks, so there was going to be a touch of rustiness and mistakes were going to happen. I think the most important thing about that first match was that we showed that a pattern was starting to develop in our play, that we were patient and we were able to take our chances. Everyone was watching how the tour was going to kick off and wondering whether we had enough ability to challenge the Springboks.

It's very difficult not to read too much into that game, but there were definitely some positive signs there: Robert Howley showed particularly impressive form; the line-out functioned reasonably well; and Jerry Guscott, who scored the opening try of the tour, looked in super form. He seemed to gel quite well with Will Greenwood who also looked impressive and, although we didn't have things all our own way in the first half, there were enough signs there that we were reasonably in control. We pulled away in the last 20 minutes which showed anyone who had harboured any doubts about us being overplayed and overworked that those doubts could be put to rest – we were clearly in good shape and extremely fit.

We came through in the last twenty minutes and effectively killed off the game with a succession of tries: Will Greenwood scored; Tony Underwood came on for a score; Jerry Guscott got another try and Doddy Weir got one. So, in the end, we ran out comfortable winners. Obviously, there had been a period when things were looking a little bit worrying, but again the patience and the ability to show some sort of pattern had come together. The most important thing was that we had won and got the tour off to a winning start. South Africa is a very difficult country to play in, and it's even more difficult when you're not winning. You have to win, and the first four games were clearly the only chance we were going to get to develop a style, an identity, a pattern which was going to carry us through the tougher games leading into the Test series. I think for the first time in Lions history, we managed to complete the first game without losing anyone to injury, which again was a plus.

Obviously, the players who hadn't been involved were itching to get out and play. In terms of my own form, I felt I could have played better, but I was reasonably happy. It was just one of those games for me when every time I ran, every time I caught up with the ball, it just seemed to go to someone else. Sometimes you have those games. You're working hard but it's not quite coming your way. But I was reasonably happy. The general feeling was that we'd had a good week, and a good win, but no one was getting carried away because there were twelve extremely hard matches to come. However, until everyone's got a game under their belt a tour's never really under way.

Eastern Province XV 9 British Lions 41

Eastern Province XV	*British Lions*
T van Rensburg	N Jenkins (Pontypridd)
H Pedro	I Evans (Llanelli)
R van Jaarsveld	J Guscott (Bath)
H Le Roux	W Greenwood (Leicester)
D Kayser	N Beal (Northampton)
K Ford	G Townsend (Northampton)

C Alcock	R Howley (Cardiff)
W Enslin	T Smith (Watsonians)
J Kirsten	K Wood (Harlequins)
D Saayman	J Leonard (Harlequins)
A du Preez	D Weir (Newcastle)
K Wiese	S Shaw (Bristol)
M Webber	L Dallaglio (Wasps)
S Scott-Young	R Hill (Saracens)
J Greeff	S Quinnell (Richmond)

Scorers
Eastern Province XV. Try: Kayser. Penalties: van Rensburg (2).
British Lions. Tries: Guscott (2), Greenwood, Underwood, Weir.
Penalties: Jenkins (2). Conversions: Jenkins (5).

Replacements
Eastern Province XV: K Ford replaced by R Fourie (41 minutes), M Webber replaced by M van der Merwe.
British Lions: K Wood replaced by B Williams (Richmond; 67), I Evans replaced by T Underwood (Newcastle; 67), D Weir replaced by J Davidson (London Irish; 72).

28 MAY 1997

Border 14 British Lions 18

We left the following day in a fairly low-key fashion and arrived in East London, a place which bears no resemblance to its namesake I can assure you. It's a fairly deserted place and the weather was even worse than it had been in Port Elizabeth.

Unfortunately, it seemed that this part of the world had experienced more rain in the last few days than they'd had in the entire winter of the previous year, which meant a wet pitch. It was immediately apparent that things were going to be very difficult, and that, in a certain sense, was a tremendous anticlimax for the selected players. The tour had got off to a huge start and I had been very fortunate to be selected for that opening game because it was played in brilliant sunshine on a rock hard pitch and we were all able to display our full range of talent. It had been perfect free-flowing rugby which enabled us to throw down the challenge to the selectors, to show them exactly what we were capable of. However, the guys who got picked for the second game weren't able to compete on the same playing field, they weren't able to display their array of talents. It was always going to be a much closer game; it was going to have to be played a lot tighter, and I think that a little frustration showed in the performance. Although Border naturally raised their game because they were playing the Lions there is no doubt that the conditions helped to level things out.

It was also clear that we were going to become increasingly frustrated with the provincial referees. To put it mildly, there was a tremendous amount of difference in interpretation between what we felt was a penalty and what they felt was a penalty. However, this was something we had discussed in Weybridge: discipline was going to be paramount if we were to be successful and, although I have argued with enough of them, I have never seen a referee change his mind. This wasn't the place to start arguing with a South African referee. It was a game which started very well and the ambition was still there from the Eastern Province game. When John Bentley scored a try in the right-hand corner it looked as if, despite the conditions, it was going to be a festival. But unfortunately that was about the only smile we had on our faces during the first half. Border played very simple in-your-face rugby and tackled as you would expect from a team that had been given the chance to play the Lions. As the game went on, it had that ominous feel about it. Although Mark Regan scored a try in the second half, we never managed to pull away and they got another try followed by a couple of penalties. They were winning as the game entered the final ten-minute period and it was really touch and go. It would have been catastrophic if we had lost to a side like Border. These first couple of games were a real chance to improvise and winning them was critical, not just to the outcome of the tour but in terms of the players' confidence.

Another thing that was fairly obvious was that Paul Grayson, who had an injury problem before he came on tour, was not operating at 100% and that was reflected in his kicking, something that was normally immaculate. Therefore, we made a few changes. Matt Dawson came on and we managed to get ourselves into an attacking position. We got a line-out in their 22; we had to win it. We drove over and Rob Wainwright got the crucial, all-important try which saved our blushes.

That late try was a defining moment of the tour. Everyone now had a game under their belt and there was a tremendous amount of relief. However, because of the appalling conditions – the game probably wouldn't have been played in the UK – there was still the feeling that the guys had not had the perfect opportunity to demonstrate their skills.

One potential hiccup was the injury to Scott Gibbs. He was taking the ball up field on one of his bulldozing runs when he looked to fall over very awkwardly on his ankle. The injury looked a lot worse than it actually turned out to be and fortunately the X-rays later showed that he had only damaged his ankle ligaments and not broken anything. The diagnosis was that it was going to be ten days to two weeks before he would be fully operational. That was sufficiently good news to keep him on board which was a tremendous relief – to lose a player like Scott after only the second game would have been a huge blow. However, unfortunately it did become evident over the next few days that Paul Grayson was going to have to leave. It's never pleasant for any player to have to go home, but these things happen on tour and you have to get over them.

The next day, those who had played against Border rested at a gym called the Health and Racket Club. There are a number of these throughout South Africa and it was team policy that this period of rest would follow each game. The rest of us went out and trained. Then we departed for Cape Town which, for me, is the best city in South Africa. We were relieved to still have an unbeaten record but this next challenge was going to be altogether different.

Border 14 British Lions 18

Border	British Lions
R Bennett	T Stimpson (Newcastle)
K Hilton-Green	J Bentley (Newcastle)
G Hechter	A Bateman (Richmond)
K Malotana	S Gibbs (Swansea)
A Classen	T Underwood (Newcastle)
G Miller	P Grayson (Northampton)
J Bradbrook	A Healey (Leicester)
H Kok	G Rowntree (Leicester)
R van Zyl	M Regan (Bristol)
D du Preez	D Young (Cardiff)
S Botha	D Weir (Newcastle)
J Gehring	J Davidson (London Irish)
M Swart	R Wainwright (Watsonians)
A Botha	N Back (Leicester)
A Fox	E Miller (Leicester)

Scorers
Border. Try: Classen. Penalties: Miller (3).
British Lions. Tries: Bentley, Regan, Wainwright. Penalty: Stimpson.

Replacements
British Lions: S Gibbs replaced by A Tait (Newcastle; 43 minutes), A Healey replaced by M Dawson (Northampton; 54), D Young replaced by P Wallace (Saracens; 67).

31 MAY 1997

Western Province 21 British Lions 38

Western Province were an accomplished side with a great history, clearly a step up from Eastern Province and Border. It was going to be a much bigger test for us. James Small and Dick Muir, both influential provincial players who had played for Natal, had moved to Western Province. They also had a number of other highly experienced players and a good up-and-coming player in Percy Montgomery, who was being spoken about as a future Springbok.

We stayed in the Holiday Inn Garden Court in Newlands which has a view of the ground. Before we could get down to the serious business of playing rugby, we had to fulfil an official duty and attend a formal reception. So we all put on our smart new blazers, our uniform or our number ones as we liked to call it, and went to the British High Commission to meet the local dignitaries. It was a good night which, through the usual storytelling and messing around, gave us the opportunity to enhance our team spirit.

Every game saw a new combination of players and so the team was changed again. Barry Williams came in at hooker and we had Graham Rowntree and Jason Leonard at prop. Martin Johnson was playing his first game so it was the first time the Lions would run out with their official captain. It was a bit of a joke that Barry Williams was the token Welshman in an English pack and he got a bit of stick from his teammates. But we were all Lions and we were all in it together. People looking on would perhaps have viewed the selection as typical, a fairly obvious choice: Robert Howley and Gregor Townsend as the half-back combination; Jerry Guscott to feature prominently; Ieuan Evans on one wing. We were trying all sorts of combinations whilst still trying to make sure that there was enough strength to win the game. I valued playing in Cape Town because, if I was going to go on and get selected for the series, it was a chance to get a feeling for playing at Newlands, to experience the atmosphere and the environment prior to the first Test. It was important that the Lions won this game – to come back to Newlands to play the first Test after having won against Western Province would be a real confidence booster.

We started very well, probably the best start we'd had so far. Tim Stimpson was in there as the number one goal kicker at the start of the game. He had never played in that kind of intense atmosphere before and there were obvious questions as to whether he was going to kick his goals. He provided the answers within the first couple of minutes of the game. He went on and kicked superbly throughout the entire game. Alan Tait scored a try in the left-hand corner and we kicked a goal, but then Western Province came back at us and showed that they weren't going to be any pushover. One element of our game that we found very encouraging was the movement that we gave the ball; we were really throwing it around and spreading and stretching Western Province, which was perhaps something that they hadn't expected. Ring rustiness had stopped us doing that in the first game, and the weather conditions had stopped us doing it in the second game. I don't think anyone really expected to see this kind of attacking, positive rugby from the Lions and, as a consequence, I think we took Western Province by surprise.

One worrying sign, however, was our scrummaging – we were being shoved all over the place. I don't think that this was because they were technically superior, but rather that it was a result of the difficulties caused by playing different combinations of forwards for each game. I know some people may say that we had seven Englishmen in the pack, seven guys who had played together, and there could be no excuse for being out-scrummaged on the day. To a certain extent they are quite right, but for one reason or another it was happening and it was keeping Western Province in the game.

At half time we discussed what was going wrong. The scrummage was a worrying aspect but everything else was functioning reasonably well: the restarts were good, the tackling in particular looked good, we were fairly solid around the fringes, the line-outs were working well and the backs were running well. We just had to keep playing and keep believing. At 21–21, Western Province had the chance to seize the initiative and really go for it but, as had happened in the first two games, we then started to come good in the last quarter of the match. Our fitness was beginning to tell and we started pulling away from the opposition. We got a wonderful break by Rob Howley which put Ieuan Evans in the right-hand corner. Then Richard Hill managed to get his toe onto a loose pass from a scrum and John Bentley scored in the other corner. The game finished 38–21 in our favour, and we had put in a good all-round performance against quality opposition. We felt they were one of the top six provincial sides in South Africa.

The challenge had been laid down and we had responded well to it. We were unbeaten, the signs were encouraging, and the most important thing, psychologically, was that we had won at Newlands, where we would play the first Test. A significant win indeed. Confidence was high and we felt that we were reasonably back in line and that things were going according to plan. By way of celebration we enjoyed a good night sampling some of Cape Town's bars and restaurants, and we all looked forward to sampling some more on our return.

Western Province 21 British Lions 38

Western Province	*British Lions*
J Swart	T Stimpson (Newcastle)
J Small	I Evans (Llanelli)
R Fleck	A Tait (Newcastle)
R Muir	J Guscott (Bath)
S Berridge	J Bentley (Newcastle)
P Montgomery	G Townsend (Northampton)
S Hatley	R Howley (Cardiff)
G Pagel	G Rowntree (Leicester)
A Paterson	B Williams (Richmond)
K Andrews	J Leonard (Harlequins)
F van Heerden	M Johnson (Leicester)
L Louw	S Shaw (Bristol)
R Brink	L Dallaglio (Wasps)
C Krige	R Hill (Saracens)
A Aitken	T Rodber (Northampton)

Scorers
Western Province. Tries: Pagel, Andrews, Fleck. Penalties: Swart.
British Lions. Tries: Bentley (2), Evans, Tait. Penalties: Stimson (4).
Conversions: Stimpson (3).

Replacements
Western Province: R Muir replaced by L Koen (57 minutes), G Pagel replaced by T van der Linde (60), C Krige replaced by B Skinstad.
British Lions: T Rodber replaced by S Quinnell (62), A Tait replaced by W Greenwood (72).

4 JUNE 1997

Mpulalanga 14 British Lions 64

We flew to Johannesburg before taking a short coach journey to Pretoria where we booked into the Holiday Inn Crowne Plaza. We were to stay there for the next eleven days which was to be the longest stay in any one place over the entire tour. During that time we would have some of the toughest games we were ever likely to play. Pretoria is far different from Cape Town in that there is not a great deal to do. Fortunately, the hotel was reasonably good, and we got down to some serious training at Loftus Versfeld Stadium, the home of Northern Transvaal Blue Bulls.

We were now at altitude, which made a difference. It was also getting to that stage where people had picked up knocks and, although they weren't serious enough to go home, training was being slightly disrupted.

One of our core values was that the whole squad would lend their support to whichever fifteen players had been selected at any given time and the need for this approach became evident on the Monday. Jim Telfer, whose job was to ensure that the scrummage was good enough to combat the South Africans, was very concerned. He had obviously had very little sleep since the poor scrummaging performance against Western Province and, before our scheduled training session, he called all the forwards in to a meeting. Basically, he had a go at the entire squad and, to be honest, he had every right to because we had let ourselves down. He reminded people of a few home truths and said that now we were in South Africa, we had to think like South Africans, we had to be South Africans, we could not afford to be

British anymore. He did not want to hear any moaning or any excuses about referees. We had to get on with the job. We were here to play and we had to get out and do the business. He came up with some interesting comparisons, calling us typical British holidaymakers who were looking only for the sun, fish and chips and pubs. The message was clear. Our scrummaging wasn't up to scratch, it had to be up to scratch, and we would be working on it morning, noon and night if that was what it would take to win.

Everyone remained very silent during the meeting, while he was spitting teeth. It wasn't a quiet session. He took it very, very personally. Jim Telfer, for those who haven't met him, gets incredibly engrossed in rugby. He was a super player. He was a British Lion himself and expects very high standards, he models his coaching and the play he wants from his forwards very much on the New Zealand approach. He expects those standards to be reached and, clearly, they hadn't been up to then. He is so enthusiastic about it, he's a perfectionist, and he wants things done properly.

People were now saying that our backs looked good, they were running great lines, they were throwing a lot of width on the ball, they had a lot of pace out wide, Jerry Guscott was in superb form – but they weren't going to get any balls. The Springbok forwards were going to eat our forwards for dinner. That was the general feeling, and Telfer took it very personally. The South Africans pride themselves on their scrummage, and there was already talk about that particular area being a significant advantage for the Springboks. When we came out of the meeting nobody was under any illusions as to the way forward. And we had the game against Mpumalanga to think about.

There were a few injuries but the squad, fortunately, had enough versatility to cope with that and Neil Jenkins moved up to stand off. He had played full back in his opening match so I think the selectors were giving everyone a chance to play in different positions. Rodber was captain, the fourth captain in four games, which also broke with tradition. The management were saying that there was no mid-week side, that they picked a captain as they saw fit.

Although knocks were being picked up and causing one or two problems, I wasn't selected for the Wednesday game so some of us went off to the gym and did our own training session, still working very hard. We had a senior players' meeting in which Martin Johnson put together a group of players who he felt should talk to the management once a week on any issues affecting the players. The group comprised Jason Leonard, Ieuan Evans and Rob Wainwright. We talked about tickets: were tickets going to be available for players, not only at the provincial games but also at the Test matches? What was going to be done for the girlfriends and wives? We also discussed training issues, what we felt worked well and what we felt needed fine tuning, we talked about the general mood in the camp and asked if anyone was having any problems – various issues like that. I think that it was all very helpful because it was a two-way process – the management got our feedback, and we got theirs.

That helps to keep the right balance within the team. We were pushing for more free time; we already felt that we were training very hard. We were training for two and a half hours every day, sometimes two training sessions a day, and the feedback from the players suggested that they needed more free time. They weren't getting any, and when they did they were too tired to do anything.

Mpulalanga's ground, Witbank, had a very hard pitch and the conditions were very hot – an ideal opportunity for people to stake their claim for the Test side. Paul Grayson had left the tour and Mike Catt came and joined the team. Mike had been in super form in England and was unlucky not to be picked for the Lions in the first place. His performances for England in Argentina only emphasised how well he could play; he almost single-handedly won the first Test for England in Buenos Aires. It was a great relief to the management to be able to call up a player who was not only good enough to fill the Lions shirt but who was also so obviously match fit. Witbank was almost a two-hour drive from Pretoria. Those who were not involved could have stayed back and watched the game in the hotel, but we felt that it was important that we stayed together as a squad. The scrummaging was vastly improved since the Western Province game – the team had made it their task to make sure that they not only scrummaged well but also that they out-scrummaged the opposition.

Rob Wainwright scored the first three tries in less than half an hour and that obviously caused some amusement in the stand. Most of the other players were surrounding me and tapping me on the back every time Rob scored, and I kept biting to the jokes that were being thrown around. Obviously, Rob was playing extremely well, but so was everyone else in the team. There were ten tries in a 64–14 win, and 64 points against any side is a massive achievement. It was a very special performance, not just for the fact that they got the result, but more so for the manner of their performance, which was particularly pleasing. There was a lot of width, the pace and power that the team displayed was again a feature, and the team generally had a good look about them. It was a step up from before. We were definitely evolving as a team. Some of the ideas that Ian and Jim were putting across in training were clearly helping. We were merely implementing a game plan that was given to us, and really coming out on top. There was a real good feeling and we were all into tour mode at this stage – we were played four, won four, and the general feeling was that things were starting to look easy. Except for Doddy Weir.

Mpulalanga got frustrated at being totally out-classed and, realising that they were not going to win the game, they started to take retribution. There were a number of incidents and there were a number of players being targeted. Some of the home team were taking the law into their own hands. Rob Wainwright came in for a bit of unnecessary slipper on the floor, and then Doddy. The referee had already blown up and then, right in front of him, their lock stamped on his knee. It was clearly after the whistle had gone, and it was an unnecessary act of violence. That effectively ended Doddy's tour, it ended his chances of playing in the Tests. It was very sad for him and, perhaps more importantly, very sad for the team because he had been in sparkling form. Obviously, injuries do happen in rugby, particularly at that level, but the manner in which that one was picked up was totally unnecessary and was one of the worst moments, if not the worst moment, of the tour. It really put a cloud over what was otherwise a superb team performance. When one man goes down the whole squad shares that disappointment and, having already lost Paul Grayson, this was a very sad day indeed.

Mpulalanga 14 British Lions 64

Mpulalanga	*British Lions*
E Gericke	N Beal (Northampton)
J Visagie	I Evans (Llanelli)
R Pitgieter	A Bateman (Richmond)
G Gendall	W Greenwood (Leicester)
P Nel	T Underwood (Newcastle)
R van As	N Jenkins (Pontypridd)
D van Zyl	M Dawson (Northampton)
H Swart	T Smith (Watsonians)
H Kemp	K Wood (Harlequins)
A Botha	P Wallace (Saracens)
M Bosman	D Weir (Newcastle)
E van den Berg	J Davidson (London Irish)
F Rossouw	R Wainwright (Watsonians)
P Joubert	N Back (Leicester)
T Oosthuizen	T Rodber (Northampton

Scorers
Mpulalanga. Tries: Joubert (2). Conversions: van As (2).
British Lions. Wainwright (3), Underwood (2), Evans (2), Dawson, Jenkins, Beal. Conversions: Jenkins (7).

Replacements
Mpulalanga: T Oosthuizen replaced by J Beukes (73 minutes).
British Lions: K Wood replaced by M Regan (Bristol; 52), D Weir replaced by S Shaw (Bristol; 55), P Wallace replaced by D Young (Cardiff; 73).

7 JUNE 1997

Northern Transvaal 35 British Lions 30

We were now entering what would probably be the most critical stage of the tour – the next ten days were going to determine whether or not we were going to come out the other side with a team capable of taking on the Boks. The South Africans were obviously playing down our achievements and were suggesting that we hadn't really played any big team as yet. Now we were to take on three of the top provincial sides, three of the top Super Twelve sides in South Africa. We were to play Northern Transvaal and Natal in a space of seven days, which really is some tall order, but the team were very confident and things had gone well thus far. Despite the loss of Doddy, the team selected for the Northern Transvaal game was picked from reasonable strength. Eric Miller was at No. 7 – he had played a fair bit there, so it wasn't a new position to him – and Scott Quinnell and myself played in the back row. Simon Shaw and Martin Johnson played in the second row – we had the England front five – and again we were very confident about the team's chances. But the game did not go well at all.

We started very badly and got hit by a very strong, committed team. We had obviously become a little bit too complacent and we had almost lulled ourselves into a false sense of security. We played particularly badly in the first twenty minutes and we never really recovered. By the time we actually started to play some rugby and get ourselves into the game it was too late and, despite a very spirited comeback, we lost the game. We gave some soft tries away during the second half and the scrummage game let us down – it was one of the reasons why they scored a couple of the tries. But they played very well indeed. They were superbly led by Adrian Richter at No. 8 who I thought was a very talented back-row forward.

It became clear to me that if we were going to be effective in stopping attacks down the blind side then we needed to scrummage a lot better than we were. We were being wheeled in the scrum and they were attacking down the blind side and there was very little, especially with the new binding laws, that I could do about it. Of course, at the back of my mind was the thought of Joost van der Westhuizen doing the same thing – he is probably one of the fastest scrum halves in world rugby, and a key Springbok. If we were getting turned by Northern Transvaal it was an extremely worrying sign of what the Boks might be able to do.

The result against Northern Transvaal was deeply disappointing because we felt it was a game that was well within our grasp. Unfortunately, we had lost a little bit of respect for the opposition and, consequently, we didn't play as well as we should have done. However, I think it was a good thing that we lost the game because it taught us a lesson – that we couldn't relax for one minute. The quality of rugby was too good, you couldn't afford to let down your guard, we had to keep playing. Technically, we picked up a number of things; the interpretation of the laws was a lot different to what we were used to. It was clear that we were going to have to attack from deep because when you kick the ball away in the southern hemisphere it takes ten minutes to get it back again. If we were to kick it away, we needed to have a strategy which would ensure that we got it back as soon as possible. We knew that if we were going to offer a serious challenge to South Africa then we were going to have to improve the scrum significantly and, in addition, we were going to have to look at ways of attacking their scrum. If we wanted to bring our back row into the game – something that I wished to see because it was an area in which we could be extremely effective – then we were going to have to do that from a stable scrum. Against Northern Transvaal we didn't posses a stable scrum so, when we tried to do back-row moves, we paid the price. Many had said that we would fall at the first big hurdle, and we had fallen – there was a huge sense of disappointment.

Northern Transvaal 35 British Lions 30

Northern Transvaal	*British Lions*
G Bouwer	T Stimpson (Newcastle)
W Lowrens	J Bentley (Newcastle)
J Schutte	J Guscott (Bath)
D van Schalkwyk	A Tait (Newcastle)
C Steyn	T Underwood (Newcastle)
R de Marigny	G Townsend (Northampton)
C Breytenbech	R Howley (Cardiff)
L Campher	G Rowntree (Leicester)
H Tromp	M Regan (Bristol)
P Boer	J Leonard (Harlequins)
D Grobbelaar	M Johnson (Leicester)
D Badenhorst	S Shaw (Bristol)
N van der Walt	L Dallaglio (Wasps)
S Bekker	E Miller (Leicester)
A Richter	S Quinnell (Richmond)

Scorers
Northern Transvaal. Tries: van Schalkwyk (2), Steyn, Richter. Penalties: Steyn (3). Conversions: Steyn (3).
British Lions. Tries: Guscott (2), Townsend. Penalties: Stimpson (3). Conversions: Stimpson (3).

Replacements
Northern Transvaal: G Bouwer temporarily replaced by J Taljaard (37–39 minutes), W Lowrens replaced by G Esterhuizen (34), H Tromp replaced by J Brooks (45), D Grobbelaar replaced by G Laufs (39), N van der Walt replaced by R Schroeder (69).
British Lions: J Bentley replaced by S Gibbs (Swansea; 64), J Leonard replaced by D Young (Cardiff; 74).

14 JUNE 1997

Gauteng Lions 14 British Lions 20

Fran Cotton called the game against Gauteng Lions (formerly Transvaal) a defining moment. It was a game that had to be won for the momentum and the success of the tour – and all credit to those who played for doing just that. Ellis Park is a very difficult place to play, and it was a night game, something we hadn't experienced before. We were under pressure, not just the team going out to play but the entire squad, and the credibility of the tour party was at stake. It was a chance to restore pride in the identity of the Lions, to get the show back on the road, something which was badly needed.

The selected team did a magnificent job. They all played themselves into contention for the Test team with particularly notable performances from Paul Wallace, Jeremy Davidson and the back row of Rodber, who captained the side, Wainwright and Back. It was really three individual moments of brilliance that won the game for the Lions. We had absorbed the pressure early on in the first half, done an incredible amount of tackling, and the game was finely balanced at half time, there was nothing in it. And then, the first individual moment of brilliance, Bentley's try. The ball came from a ruck and Neil Jenkins threw out a long ball to John, still in his own half, who then went on a quite blistering run and beat seven players to score under the posts. It was one of those moments that will be remembered as one of the best tries ever scored, certainly at that level. It was a quite breathtaking piece of rugby. The South African supporters, who know a good try when they see one, were in awe. I had been wrapped in as much tension as everyone else, and I was absolutely delighted when John scored. Having taken the abuse that was ringing in my ears for large periods of the game, which was directed not only at me but at my team and the squad in general, I now had the chance to stick two fingers up at everyone in the stadium and say 'Take that'. It was a super score and it really turned the game.

Then came the other two moments. Austin Healey's try followed some superb inter-passing between the forwards, then a one-two with Will Greenwood, and then some superb acceleration with a step and a swerve round the full back, again a quite a magnificent individual try. Then there was a substitution and Neil Jenkins came on the field for Tony Underwood. The Lions got a penalty, about 40 metres out on the right-hand touchline. Neil elected to take a crack at goal and kicked a quite brilliant penalty goal that put the Lions two scores ahead. For the first time in the game the squad had a little bit of breathing space but, sure enough, Gauteng came back. They did score a try at the end, but it wasn't enough to reverse the result.

What that win did for the squad can be summed up in the fact that every single member of the tour party was there to greet the team as they came off the pitch. The show was back on the road, and this result gave us the confidence to take on Natal on the Saturday. I also think that several of the players played themselves into the Test team on that particular night.

Gauteng Lions 14 British Lions 20

Gauteng Lions	*British Lions*
D du Toit	N Beal (Northampton)
J Gillingham	J Bentley (Newcastle)
J van der Walt	J Guscott (Bath)
H Le Roux	W Greenwood (Leicester)
P Hendricks	T Underwood (Newcastle)
L van Rensburg	M Catt (Bath)
J Roux	A Healey (Leicester)
R Grau	T Smith (Watsonians)
C Rossouw	B Williams (Richmond)
K van Greuning	P Wallace (Saracens)
K Wiese	N Redman (Bath)
B Thorne	J Davidson (London Irish)
A Vos	R Wainwright (Watsonians)
P Krause	N Back (Leicester)
W Brosnihan	T Rodber (Northampton)

Scorers
Gauteng Lions. Try: Vos. Penalties: du Toit (3).
British Lions. Tries: Healey, Bentley. Penalties: Catt, Jenkins. Conversions: Jenkins (2).

Replacements
Gauteng Lions: C Rossouw replaced by J Dalton (52), R Grau replaced by B Swart (60).
British Lions: T Underwood replaced by N Jenkins (Pontypridd, 52).

14 JUNE 1997

Natal 12 British Lions 42

It was a welcome relief to get out of Pretoria but, for the past eleven days, I'd had a fantastic roommate in David Young of Cardiff. I think a lot of people were struggling in Pretoria, but he and I got on very well and we had great fun. But now it was time to move on, it was time to get back to Durban. We checked back into the luxury of the Beverly Hills Hotel – the people who had looked after us there before already knew our requirements.

Andy Keast came into his own at this particular time, he had been beavering away at the video analysis and preparing tapes of the opposition for us. His first-hand experience of Natal was crucial for this particular game. I was delighted to be selected, but I think a lot of people had provisionally put this game aside as a game which would probably feature the shadow Test team. The selectors maybe felt that they didn't want to reveal their hand too early. However, as a result of some great performances during the Gauteng game, the cat had really been thrown amongst the pigeons and had caused a lot of selection problems. I don't think the management wanted to give South Africa any advantage by naming, or looking like they were naming, the Test team too early. We needed every edge we could get, and that was an edge. This was a chance for us to throw down the gauntlet by beating the best provincial side in South Africa on a Test pitch. We needed to see a solid display from the forwards against a top side like Natal, which would give us the confidence to take on the Boks. And we saw just that.

I feel that it wasn't just the matter of victory that was important, but also the manner in which we won the game – we won with a very limited amount of fuss. It was a very workman-like, professional performance against Natal, but it showed that there was no way we could go into a contest with South Africa without Neil Jenkins. His goal kicking was simply immaculate. He scored 24 points, six penalties and three conversions – virtually every chance he was given. He kicked himself into the Test team.

Once we had managed to put a bit of breathing space between us and them we started to relax and we began to play the kind of rugby which had not been seen in some of the other provincial games. And we scored some good tries. Two came from kicks ahead, one by Townsend and the other from Catt. But we lost Howley early on, after only twelve minutes, which was a cruel blow. I was close to that incident, and players know when other players have had a bad injury. You could see Rob was bad and would not take part in the rest of the game – he had dislocated his shoulder. Matt Dawson came on and, because it was so early on in the game, he was able to get straight into the action and he played very well indeed. We tried to put Howley to the back of our minds, tried to get on with playing as well as we could – we would worry about the implications of that injury afterwards. Things went very well for us. I felt that, defensively, we tackled superbly, in particular Gibbs and Bateman, and the back row went very well. It felt like the best combination we had had up till then. Personally, I felt much more involved in the game; I was getting myself into good positions and getting on to loose balls. Things worked very well.

There was a big crowd that day and Natal, nicknamed the Sharks, were out to eat the Lions. And, really, we despatched them with the minimum amount of fuss. The scrummaging was superb for the first time. We actually found a technique that worked; we were able to take the scrums at whatever position we wanted, both offensively and defensively. The restarts were superb. We were winning our restarts, and we were winning their restarts, and it was a much more confident performance up front.

If I had to give that game a mark it would be eight out of ten for a good win, and perhaps that was something which we hadn't achieved before then. At that moment people actually realised that it wasn't going to be such an easy show for South Africa – it was going to be a much closer series than they had imagined.

I suppose any coach would tell you that he would rather have all his squad playing well, and causing a few selection problems, than have only the chosen few in good shape. That was exactly what was happening on this tour, and the Test team that most people would have put down on paper before the series began was now in danger of being torn apart. But that's exactly what we wanted. No one was guaranteed a place and I think that was very healthy. The manner of the win in Durban had, I think, given us the confidence that we needed to go on and really take on the South Africans. We came out of that week in pretty good shape. We had now played six and won five, which was a good effort.

We still had a few injury problems but Scott Quinnell was now replaced by Tony Diprose who had just earned his first cap for England and was flying over from Argentina to join us in Cape Town. Nigel Redman had also been playing in Argentina and he was Weir's replacement. No one was unhappy about him becoming a British Lion. He has been a great servant of the game and played many seasons for Bath, and many years for England. It was good to see him on tour. Obviously Howley had to be replaced as well and Kyran Bracken, who was England's scrum half in Argentina, was the choice, which meant an all-English competition for that position.

Natal 12 British Lions 42

Natal	*British Lions*
G Lawless	N Jenkins (Pontypridd)
S Payne	I Evans (Llanelli)
J Thompson	A Bateman (Richmond)
P Muller	S Gibbs (Swansea)
J Joubert	A Tait (Newcastle)
H Scriba	G Townsend (Northampton)
R du Preez	R Howley (Cardiff)
O Le Roux	T Smith (Watsonians)
J Allan	K Wood (Harlequins)
R Kempson	D Young (Cardiff)

N Wegner	M Johnson (Leicester)
J Slade	S Shaw (Bristol)
W van Heerden	L Dallaglio (Wasps)
W Fyvie	R Hill (Saracens)
D Kriese	E Miller (Leicester)

Scorers
Natal. Penalties: Lawless (4).
British Lions. Tries: Townsend, Catt, Dallaglio. Penalties: Jenkins (6).
Conversions: Jenkins (3). Dropped goal: Townsend.

Replacements
Natal: O Le Roux replaced by J Smit (67 minutes), W van Heerden replaced by R Strudwick (29).
British Lions: R Howley replaced by M Dawson (Northampton; 12), M Johnson temporarily replaced by R Wainwright (Watsonians; 25–33), A Bateman replaced by M Catt (66), T Smith replaced by J Leonard (67).

17 JUNE 1997

Emerging Springboks 22 British Lions 51

We arrived in Cape Town on the Sunday after a long day travelling, longer than we expected. But we still maintained the one-meal-with-the-squad plan and went out to a restaurant called Blues in Camps Bay, which was a particularly pleasant experience.

We put out a strong side for the game against the Emerging Springboks – it was important, especially after having had a good performance against Natal that we kept the momentum up and kept the pressure on South Africa. We'd won the last two crucial big games but here were a number of younger, aspiring would-be Springboks who would be trying to beat us, so it was a key game. It was also everyone's last chance to secure a Test place. But it was a game that we were never really in danger of losing. The guys played tremendously well and scored very quickly. Graham Rowntree scored a try on the wing which epitomised the type of rugby we were playing. You would never see him careering in off the left wing for a try in the corner at

Leicester. Some of the handling and the deft touches were superb. Nick Beal played particularly well and Tony Diprose fitted in well too, so it was altogether very encouraging.

The Natal game had given everyone the edge they needed and we were now moving into the most important part of the tour, the first Test. The fight for places was more intense than anyone had anticipated. The guys that played in that game at Wellington did their chances no harm at all. Neil Back had a super game and was voted man of the match, and it really gave us the springboard we needed. We woke up on Wednesday morning in confident mood.

Emerging Springboks 22 British Lions 51

Emerging Springboks	British Lions
M Smith (Orange Free State)	T Stimpson (Newcastle)
D Kayser (Eastern Province)	N Beal (Northampton)
P Montgomery (Western Province)	A Bateman (Richmond)
M Hendricks (Boland)	W Greenwood (Leicester)
P Treu (South West Districts)	J Bentley (Newcastle)
L van Rensburg (Gauteng)	M Catt (Bath)
J Adlam (North West)	A Healey (Leicester)
R Kempson (Natal)	G Rowntree (Leicester)
D Santon (Boland)	M Regan (Bristol)
N du Toit (Boland)	J Leonard (Harlequins)
B Els (Orange Free State)	N Redman (Bath)
R Opperman (Orange Free State)	J Davidson (London Irish)
W Brosnihan (Gauteng Lions)	R Wainwright (Watsonians)
P Smit (Griqualand West)	N Back (Leicester)
J Coetzee (Orange Free State)	A Diprose (Saracens)

Scorers
Emerging Springboks. Tries: Brosnihan, Goosen, Treu. Penalty: Smith. Conversions: Smith, Montgomery.
British Lions. Tries: Rowntree, Beal (3), Stimpson, Catt. Penalties: Stimpson (3). Conversions: Stimpson (6).

Replacements
Emerging Springboks: J Adlam replaced by K Myburgh (Griqualand West; 11 minutes), L van Rensburg replaced by M Goosen (Boland; 22), Smith replaced by K Malotana (Border; 65), R Kempson replaced by L Campher (Northern Transvaal).

21 JUNE 1997

South Africa 16 British Lions 25

We went to Stellenbosch for training, once in the morning and once in the afternoon. We felt it would be nice to have a change of atmosphere, a change of environment – and we obviously wanted to have a look at the vineyards. So we went up to the vineyards and trained at Stellenbosch Rugby Club – a very famous club – and had a good session there. The way the team was to be announced had been determined at Weybridge – an envelope under the door two days before the game would tell a player if he had been selected or not. I was rooming with Tony Diprose at the time who, having just arrived on tour, wasn't really expecting to be in the team. I have played and toured with Tony a number of times and we get on very well. He had no hesitation in congratulating me when I was selected for the first Test.

The envelope had arrived quite late at night, but I didn't pick it up till I woke at about seven in the morning. I was highly delighted and more than a little relieved because as much as people say that you were probably always going to play, I don't subscribe to that view. The competition was intense. Rob Wainwright was playing particularly well. He'd been in excellent form. Tim Rodber had led the side magnificently when asked to. Eric Miller was also in good form. He had played a super game against Natal. The contest between Neil Back and Richard Hill was one which would have had most judges reaching for their calculators. So it was going to be an intriguing selection, and by no means a foregone conclusion. As we prepared for training, it became clear who had been picked . . .

People started to talk to each other, ask each other. There were some very interesting selections, notably Paul Wallace, Jeremy Davidson and Tom Smith. Everyone had suggested that the English front five were going to be the Test choice. The hooker spot was keenly contested – Keith Wood, Barry

Williams and Mark Regan, very difficult to pull them apart. I think that probably gave the selectors a lot of heartache. Martin Johnson told me that the selection meetings had gone on for a long time and there had been a lot of argument between the people involved. They obviously weren't able to make up their minds easily. Alan Tait played his way into the Test side as well. He played very well at centre and on the wing. A lot of people probably wouldn't have thought beforehand that he'd be the left wing for the first Test.

The selection kept a lot of people guessing, not just people within the squad but people outside as well and, most importantly, the South Africans themselves. They were going to play yet another combination of players and, having geared themselves up to play against certain individuals, those selections probably threw them off slightly. It was pretty clear that the coaches had put their necks on the chopping block with certain selections, and had they not come through there would have been some very awkward questions to face. Unfortunately Eric Miller, who had had a super game against Natal, had gone down with flu. The team was an interesting gamble but, because everyone had so far played so well, I'm sure they could have put any fifteen squad members in that team and they would all have given exactly the same.

We were now reaching our peak. We realised what our potential was and we weren't trying to play beyond our capability. We had now won six out of seven matches so we knew how to win games, and we knew how this particular team could win. Everyone in South Africa thought we were going to lose, except us. We knew that we had the ability to take on anyone. We were very, very confident. We obviously realised it was going to be yet another step up from any game we had played up to then. It was going to be a huge game. South Africa had a warm-up game against Tonga but they weren't really tested, it was a bit of a nothing contest, and it probably gave them a feeling that they were a lot better than they were. Critically, none of their team had had first-hand experience of the British Lions because, for once, they had chosen to withdraw from provincial games, so there was a lot of complacency and arrogance. Had they played against the Lions they would have realised that we were strong and tough, we were hard and fast and mean enough to beat them – that would have stopped any complacency. That was another edge we had.

Things went very well in training. It was a new combination so there were things to work on. For instance, Paul Wallace hadn't lifted Martin Johnson at the front of the line-out, so that was something to work on for that week. There was a fair bit to go through, but we got on with it very well and the guys who hadn't been selected supported us very well. On the Friday it was decided that the 21 selected players needed a break, a change of scenery. So on the Friday afternoon we, along with our coaches, went along to the botanical gardens where we had a cream tea together. Wandering around the gardens and enjoying that meal together worked wonders in terms of relaxation and increasing team spirit.

Leading up to the Test, Andy Keast again came into his own. He prepared videos on units within the South African team, and on each individual within the team. We'd been through the game plan all week and we knew how we wanted to play. Perhaps more important is the fact that we also understood their game plan. Through these sessions we could see how South Africa would play against us. We revised this information on the Friday night. It was important that we fully understood the enemy – and knew what it would take to stop them. As in any good team, their spine was with positions 2, 8, 9, 10 and 15. And it was clear that their game plan revolved around 8, 9, 10 and 15. They were key players, three of them from Natal. Van der Westhuizen had a primary role in the team and the link with Henry Honiball at fly half was a crucial area. And we felt if we could stop them playing in that area, particularly Honiball because he either played very flat or very deep –

we were in business. If he played deep he was going to kick, but nine times out of ten he takes the ball very flat and he likes to feed runners either side of him, usually Teichmann or Kruger, so we highlighted an area where we felt we had an advantage.

If we were going to win we had to close them down there. We had to ensure that our back row, and our inside midfield, were strong enough to stop, disrupt and upset their game plan. And that meant stopping Kruger and Teichmann in their tracks and putting pressure on Honiball – and quite early on. With the scrummage we now had a formula which, although it would never dominate the South Africans, would allow us to contest our own ball. We had a formula which we felt would disrupt them, would stop them doing the things they wanted to do off the scrum. And going into the game, that is exactly what happened.

The anticipation of playing in the first Test was unbelievable and when we actually got out there I was very emotional, especially when the anthem was being sung. The fact that we had won at Newlands before really benefited us. We had been in the changing room, we'd been in the stadium, we'd been there and we'd won. Nothing to worry about. The game went very well indeed. We closed them down in the areas we wanted to. Some of the tackling was sensational – Gibbs and Rodber in particular – and van der Westhuizen couldn't really get any momentum going with his little swipes down the blind side. Teichmann was marshalled very well and we closed down the space around Honiball, so they couldn't get their running game going which forced them into making a lot of uncharacteristic mistakes. Joubert was looking unsteady at the back and there were a lot of handling errors. We were tackling with an intensity and an aggression which perhaps can only be found in Test matches and we really put doubts in their mind. Having scored so many points against Tonga, I don't think they quite knew how to respond when things started going very wrong.

We were ahead at half time. The important thing was that we had taken our chances when we had them. We had the belief we could go on and win the match but there was no doubt that South Africa were going to come back at us. Scott Gibbs missed one of the few tackles he missed all tour and Teichmann got through to allow Russell Bennett to score in the corner. But the belief we had in the team meant that we were straight back at them, straight back in there. There was a point when we were losing the game but we had a scrum just inside their 22 and we felt that if we were going to make an impression we would have to score then. We called a move – Tim Rodber called a solo ball. He was in charge of back row moves. We just got the right hand we wanted on the scrum, and Matt Dawson did the move. It meant the scrum half picking the ball up and running off on his own, so we had to get the necessary wheel. I'd learned from the Northern Transvaal game that if you do get wheeled, on a blind side, it becomes very difficult to tackle the scrum half. It doesn't matter how good you are, you are not going to catch him – and Kruger couldn't catch Dawson. He got outside Kruger and set off down the wing. It didn't really look like there was a lot of space but he threw an overhead dummy and the whole South African defence just froze, Teichmann and Joubert in particular, and Matt kept running to score a superb individual try.

It was a super dummy and he did just what van der Westhuizen might have done. Any doubts that we were missing Rob Howley had been firmly put to bed at that stage. Matt really played a super game and that moment of individual brilliance will be remembered for ever. That try put us in front. Our timing was impeccable, it was the right time to score. It was coming to the last quarter of the game and we were finishing strongly, as we had done in all the other games. And once the South Africans went behind, they started to panic – their heads dropped and they started to run. This wasn't what was supposed to happen. These Lions were supposed to be out of sight by now – that was clearly what they thought.

We knew that we had to win the first Test to stand any chance of winning the series. And we knew that once we got our noses in front there was no way they were going to win the game. We made them attack from deep and we were tackling so well that they weren't able to get any momentum. We kept forcing mistakes. They were making so many handling errors, so many bad kicks, and eventually we scored another try which effectively killed the game off. Scott Gibbs took the ball on, Tim Rodber made a lovely pass to Neil Jenkins who then put Alan Tait in the corner, and that was the end of it.

The support we had in Cape Town was superb. The crowd was fantastic and it really helped us to achieve what was a famous victory. We now wanted to go on and win the series, but we had to keep everything in perspective. Martin Johnson was particularly adamant that no one should get carried away. When we got back to the hotel we were told to go out and enjoy yourselves, to have a few beers – we deserved it, we'd had a great victory. However, we were also reminded that our mission was not yet over and everyone – and they meant everyone because next week's team could be completely different – would do well to keep this thought in the backs of their minds. We needed to ensure that we won the next game, and the one after that as well. So, just a little word of caution, which was accepted and taken on board by everyone. Although we went out to enjoy ourselves in Cape Town, we didn't split up. We all went out together for a meal, to the same place we'd been to after we'd played Western Province. Once we'd had the meal together we slid off into groups and went out and partied a bit longer. I don't think anyone could quite believe we had won the first Test when we woke up in the morning. It was a dream come true.

Sunday was a rest day because, physically and mentally, the game had taken a hell of a lot out of us all and it was important that we got the right recovery. The other thing was that we were leaving to relocate at Durban. So it was going to be a day of rest, then one of travel. It was significant that we were going back to Durban, a place that we had visited twice before, and a place where we had won. There was no better venue for the second Test.

Sunday night saw us in different rooms, with different roommates. We spent the time reflecting on the fact that we had won. Apart from it being a major achievement, any rugby player knows that your mind dwells on the last game, at least until you shake off the effects of the inevitable knocks. Physically, it was the hardest Test match I had ever been involved in. The pressure was relentless, tension was at fever pitch. Again, it was something which the Five Nations' doesn't create. Some of the provincial games we played were harder than a lot of the Five Nations' matches, and the Test was another level higher. Martin Johnson said after the Northern Transvaal game that it was harder than any Five Nations' match he had ever been involved in, and he had won several England caps. So it gives an indication of the level we were playing at. It was certainly very tough indeed.

South Africa 16 British Lions 25

South Africa	British Lions
A Joubert (Natal)	N Jenkins (Pontypridd)
J Small (Western Province)	I Evans (Llanelli)
J Mulder (Gauteng)	J Guscott (Bath)
E Lubbe (Griqualand West)	S Gibbs (Swansea)
A Snyman (N Transvaal)	A Tait (Newcastle)
H Honiball (Natal)	G Townsend (Northampton)
J van der Westhuizen (N Transvaal)	M Dawson (Northampton)
O du Randt (Orange Free State)	T Smith (Watsonians)
N Drotske (Orange Free State)	K Wood (Harlequins)
A Garvey (Natal)	P Wallace (Saracens)
H Strydom (Gauteng)	M Johnson (Leicester)
M Andrews (Natal)	J Davidson (London Irish)
R Kruger (N Transvaal)	L Dallaglio (Wasps)
A Venter (Orange Free State)	R Hill (Saracens)
G Teichmann (Natal)	T Rodber (Northampton)

Scorers
South Africa. Tries: du Randt, Bennett. Penalties: Lubbe, Honiball.
British Lions. Tries: Dawson, Tait. Penalties: Jenkins (5).

Replacements
South Africa. E Lubbe replaced by R Bennett (Border, 41).
British Lions: T Smith replaced by J Leonard (Harlequins; 80).

24 JUNE 1997

Orange Free State 30 British Lions 52

It was being hammered home that this game, one outside the Test series, was probably going to be the hardest game we were ever likely to play, and I remembered my experience of playing there in the first game in 1994, when we got well beaten. For the first time, the Test team, those who hadn't been selected for this game, did not travel with the players to Bloemfontein. This was undoubtedly one of the main benefits of having a squad of 35 – it allowed players adequate time to recover between games.

The guys who were scheduled to play would go up and down in a day, which was something we had discussed as a group of senior players and we all felt that it would be in the team's best interests. Bloemfontein was not a place that the team wanted to hang around in particularly, so it was important they went in there, played the game and came out again. Nigel Redman was selected as captain, a tremendous honour for him. I thought it would be a very hard game in Bloemfontein. It was important to keep the squad's momentum going and the players who stayed behind in Durban knew that. So, back at the hotel, we set up a big screen in the team room and watched the game together. That gives you an indication of the team spirit that existed. No one went up to their room. We all sat there with a plate of sandwiches and a few drinks and we were glued to the game. The team put on what was probably the best performance of pure rugby in the entire tour. All credit to those players involved – it was probably the best Lions performance, and I include the Test matches, of any team in the 13 matches played out there. I think even the South Africans had to admit that it really was a dazzling display of running rugby. John Bentley got a hat trick of tries and Will Greenwood and Alan Bateman were superb in the centre. Every man who played was magnificent. The ball was all over the park, with pace and power. We were just in awe back at the hotel. A phenomenal performance, 52–30 with seven tries.

Little did we know that we had a documentary team following us, and they were there, filming us – a lot of editing was called for, I'm sure. This had been a particularly encouraging performance, one that we were very proud of, and it served to lift the tour out of top gear and into overdrive. The guys came back at two in the morning, and Eric Miller didn't even bother waking me up. There was, however, a tiny worry over Will Greenwood who had taken a really nasty bang and was unconscious for a time. It was a nasty injury, but fortunately he was OK. He finished up with a dislocated shoulder and pretty severe concussion. We were all very relieved that it wasn't any more serious and although he had played his last game on tour, he had played magnificently throughout.

Orange Free State 30 British Lions 52

Orange Free State	*British Lions*
M Smith	T Stimpson (Newcastle)
J Van Wyk	J Bentley (Newcastle)
H Muller	A Bateman (Richmond)
B Venter	W Greenwood (Leicester)
S Brink	T Underwood (Newcastle)
J de Beer	M Catt (Bath)
S Fourie	A Healey (Leicester)
D Groenewald	G Rowntree (Leicester)
C Marais	B Williams (Richmond)
W Meyer	D Young (Cardiff)
R Opperman	N Redman (Bath)
B Els	S Shaw (Wasps)
C van Rensburg	R Wainwright (Watsonians)
J Erasmus	N Back (Leicester)
J Coetzee	E Miller (Leicester)

Scorers
Orange Free State. Tries: Brink (2), de Beer. Penalties: de Beer (2).
Conversions: de Beer (3).
British Lions. Tries: Stimpson, Bentley (3), Bateman, Jenkins,
Underwood. Penalties: Stimpson (3). Conversions: Stimpson (4).

Replacements
Orange Free State: S Fourie replaced by H Jacobs (40 minutes), W
Meyer replaced by D Heymans (60).
British Lions: J Leonard temporarily replaced by G Rowntree (Leicester;
temporarily:16–20, permanently, 73). W Greenwood replaced by N
Jenkins (Pontypridd; 40).

28 JUNE 1997

South Africa 15 British Lions 18

There was no change to the Test team. We were back at
Kings Park training and again we knew we were capable of
beating South Africa. The slating they got in the press after
losing at Cape Town was astonishing. We think our press is
bad, climbing on our backs when we lose, but the South
Africans were calling for heads, they were saying the players
didn't have sufficient pride to wear the Springbok jersey and
they were creating a tidal wave of emotion, suggesting South
Africa were going to come out throwing everything at us in
that second Test.

Jim Telfer said that we had climbed Everest in Cape Town
to win the first Test and now we were going to have to get
down to do it all over again, and it was going to be even
harder. We were very aware of a South African backlash.
The message was hammered home through remembering
that, in 1994, and against all the odds, England had beaten
South Africa, really beaten them comprehensively. Maybe
England had then got a little bit complacent and thought
things were going to be as easy, but South Africa have got
far too much pride to sit back and be beaten again.
Remember also Newlands in 1994, when England were
physically intimidated. That was talked about as soon as we

won the first Test: let's not be complacent. And the other thing we remembered and talked about was the fact that, in the history of rugby, South Africa had only been beaten twice before at home. The All Blacks did it in 1996. We were on the verge of doing something very special. One final push, and we could do it.

The South Africans never look beyond themselves, and that had cost them the first Test. That's just the nature of their rugby. They play best and they examine their own performance – they're not interested in anyone else's. They want to control their own performance. By their own standards they hadn't played as well as they could, but they had played as well as they were allowed to play. We had highlighted the game plan that revolved around stopping Teichmann, Honiball and van der Westhuizen, so we did not want to change that, not at all. Same formula. The only thing we felt we wanted to do more was to retain possession, to try and keep hold of the ball a bit longer.

So the Test team was selected and we went about our training in similar fashion to what had proved successful right the way through. The guys that had played in the Free State game were buzzing and, although they hadn't been selected for the Test team, they were proud that they had achieved something very special themselves. The only disappointment was the injury to Ieuan Evans. Everything was going well when Ieuan broke down with a groin injury. Players are aware when other players have a bad injury. No one crowds the injured. As he was lying on the floor, obviously in a lot of pain, the players moved away and gave that sort of look to each other, very worried that he might be out for the rest of the tour. Ieuan, a canny, streetwise character who was in great form, had been involved in two previous Lions tours and it was unfortunate that he couldn't go on and extend his sequence of Test matches. So the stage was set for John Bentley to come in. If anyone had talked his way into the Test team, John had. He had been one of the real characters, both on and off the pitch. Before I left

England, Dean Ryan, the Newcastle captain, had said, 'You'll get on with John Bentley, he's an absolute madman' – he wasn't wrong at all, and we got on very well. John had played very well and if anyone was going to force their way into the Test team it was him. As fate would have it, he managed to get his opportunity. That was the one change, and it gave us a shift in focus – the press coverage of John Bentley's selection really gave the South Africans something to think about.

Fortunately for us, we only had the one change, but they had a lot more to consider. Some of their changes were enforced, some were optional. Their coach, Carel du Plessis, was under pressure. He was under great pressure to get back to winning ways, so he made a couple of changes. But they had problems with injuries as well. They had lost key personnel, which obviously disrupted them. They also had a few problems with their backs, a crucial area in any game and particularly so in this series. So they weren't without problems themselves.

Fran Cotton is a very superstitious person and he probably wanted to keep the same sort of rhythm and format as we'd had in the previous Test. What was successful in Cape Town should be successful in Durban – so we went to an aviary about 20 minutes' drive away, again just the 21 involved. They put on a bird show for us and we felt like six-year-olds again, but we had a good time. It was becoming a bit of a joke now – the botanical gardens last week and the bird show this week. If anyone got wind of this, we were in trouble. But it worked, it helped everyone get more relaxed, more focused, and better prepared for what was about to be the biggest rugby day of our lives. It was sometimes quite difficult to know what to do to fill a match day. The kickoff was at 5.15 pm and, having had Ella earlier in the year, I was naturally used to being up and about quite early on. Our usual practice was to go for a stroll after lunch.

On this occasion we walked round the corner to a patch

of grass outside the hotel and went through all the line-outs and all the forward moves, just so we were absolutely clear about what we were doing. Then we went back to the hotel where we changed into our tracksuits ready for the game and assembled for the final team meeting. Ian McGeechan gave a very emotional but controlled speech about how special this day was for everyone, saying that we were capable of winning and how and why we would win. It was a superb delivery – uplifting and motivational. After Fran had said his piece it was Ian's turn, a time to be alone with his players before we got on and did the business. We arrived at Kings Park in a very confident and determined mood. We knew that it was going to be a war, but we were ready for it. Again, the changing room was reasonably calm. There was no head-banging; everyone went off and into their own little rhythm, into their own little world. Some players were noisier than others, and for some the nervous tension became too much and they were physically sick. It's understandable. Then, ten minutes before kick-off, we came back together again – and in just the right frame of mind to win a Test match.

This had to be the most eagerly awaited game of the summer – South Africa had to win to keep the contest alive and this was the Lions' chance to wrap up the Test series. It was a huge day with everything at stake. During the intense build-up to the game the level of anticipation had reached mouth-watering proportions. We ran out on time and were immediately hit by the incredible atmosphere out there. The reception we got from our own supporters was quite amazing. Lions' support had grown and grown throughout the tour and here we were greeted with a wall of red, white and blue. We got ourselves into a huddle to await the South Africans, and when they emerged from the tunnel the noise reached a level that was just something else. The whole atmosphere was phenomenal, something I'd never before witnessed and I seriously doubt that I will see the like of it again. We lined up for the anthems with every Lions player holding on to each other – it was a very emotional scene.

The playing of two anthems can go on a bit, especially as we were eager to get on with it, and towards the end Scott Gibbs started firing out his orders – we were not going to take a step back, it was to be forward and at them, and we were going to win this war. We kicked off to them and, from the second that they caught the ball, their intention was obvious. They had come out with all guns firing, they were popping balls off the side, they were firing players in support – and we had no answer to it, tackle after tackle after tackle. That incessant pressure culminated in a couple of penalties in the first ten minutes, but they missed them both. Not only was this a huge relief but it was also very encouraging. We had successfully absorbed so much pressure, we hadn't touched the ball for twenty minutes, and yet they still hadn't managed to score. Seeing the opposition miss those penalties increased our self-belief, it really gave us a lift.

We managed to battle our way back up field. Neil Jenkins had a penalty chance, his first, just inside their half. He really showed them how world-class goal kicking should be done by putting it straight between the posts. He then knocked over another and we were 6–0 up. They'd had all the play, we'd only ventured into their half twice, but we'd scored six points. However, they came straight back at us again. Eventually the pressure had to tell and, after Kruger had a try disallowed, van der Westhuizen scored to make it 6–5. They had their tails up now, but they missed the conversion and that was to prove crucial later on in the game. They had a last attack just before half time and Gibbs made a try-saving tackle on Joubert which really kept us in the game. We went in at half time still holding on to that lead despite having been under the cosh for probably thirty-five of the first forty minutes. I don't think anyone could quite believe it.

Martin said a few words, Ian McGeechan said a few words and then, when things calmed down, I said a few words as well. I simply re-emphasised the fact that, although they'd thrown everything they had at us, we were ahead. We were going to go back out there and take the game to them, we would eliminate mistakes and really put on a show. Another forty minutes and we would be heroes, we would have made history. We went back onto the pitch and basically did exactly the opposite. We certainly made some costly mistakes. Within the first minute Alan Tait slipped an underhand pass out the back straight into Percy Montgomery's hand. He went through and scored a try. Having worked so hard to stay 6–5 in front, all of a sudden we were 10–6 down. We managed to claw back a penalty making it 10–9 but, almost immediately, we then gave away another try, this time to Joubert, which took us to 15–9. Instead of panicking, which we could have done, we kept our cool and took heart from the fact that there was still twenty minutes left. There was still time.

They missed the conversion. We were still in the game. We still had the belief that we could get up there, that we could get something. Just one converted try would put us back in front. But South Africa had us under pressure for about the next ten minutes and we just couldn't get out of our own half. I knew if South Africa had scored at that point then the game would have effectively been over. But, somehow, we kept them out. There was some phenomenal tackling going in all over the place and then, eventually, we turned things round. We got up into their half where they gave a penalty away, one which we successfully took on. We then got a second penalty, and it was over to Neil Jenkins. He was just so cool under pressure and, against a wall of sound, he put the ball straight between the posts. A phenomenal display under extremely difficult conditions.

We knew that, every time we got up there, if they conceded a penalty we would earn the points. The difference between the sides was the discipline – one of our core values that had been highlighted early on in the tour. We only gave away eight penalties in the whole game whereas they gave away eighteen, and that was the essential difference between us. In fact, during the second half we only gave away one penalty which, given the highly pressurised conditions, probably proved to be the key factor. South Africa missed four chances at goal, but they only missed as many chances as they were allowed to have. We didn't give them one kickable penalty in the second half and that was absolutely crucial. In their half they infringed, and Jenkins made them pay for that. His fifth kick brought us to 15–15.

We were still under pressure but then Keith Wood put in a long punt down the field and all of a sudden, with five minutes to go, we had a line-out on the edge of their 22.

It was our throw but we felt that, whatever the call, Jeremy Davidson was going to win the ball. We got a good drive, a fantastic drive really, and Dawson fed Townsend who took the ball really flat and was tackled. Fortunately we recycled the ball the right way and Dawson picked out Guscott, the only guy left available in the back line. He hit a superb drop goal. I've seen him hit drop goals before but that particular one was just great. He didn't have a lot of time to get it down and up, especially as he had Teichmann and Honiball breathing down his neck, but he showed remarkable confidence and his usual accuracy to do just that.

With only five minutes remaining, the South Africans went into a frenzied panic. It was knife-edge stuff. They obviously desperately wanted to win, and they were given the opportunity to do so with a scrum in front of the posts. They probably could have gone for the drop goal and tied the game up but they had to go for the try, that's their mentality, and we defended superbly. Then, when they kicked the ball dead, it was our 22 drop-out. I remember asking the referee, Didier Mene, how long was left and he said that he would blow the whistle after the 22. So I turned to Neil and told him to kick the ball off the pitch. In the event, Neil had to call it twice but, after the ball had gone off the pitch for the second time, the referee blew the whistle. The score was 18–15 to the Lions. It was over.

Now, the emotion was just indescribable. I just wanted to

hug every member of the team on the pitch, sympathise with the opposition briefly, and then hug every member of the squad. Everyone came down onto the pitch, the other squad members and the management, and we all celebrated together. This was a true reflection of the way the whole tour had been conducted – this wasn't just a victory for the 15 players, it was a victory for all 47 members of the touring party.

South Africa couldn't believe that they had lost. No one had given us a chance before the tour. We'd had it rammed down our throats that we stood no chance against a side as good as South Africa, that we would never be able to emulate the great Lions of 1974. Nobody had given us any credit and nobody had rated us right the way throughout the tour. It had been our self-belief, our discipline and intelligence, our attitude and desire that had won through in the end. That and the touch of genius from Jerry Guscott. He's a superb player who has enjoyed a tremendous amount of success with both club and country – and with the Lions – but I'm sure he would agree that nothing can compare with that moment – his drop goal, the final whistle, the winning of the Test series. South Africa had been beaten in a home series for only the third time ever, and we had done it. There was so much mixed emotion – tears, shock, happiness, disbelief – and it was fantastic. That's what top-level sport is all about, and we had worked so hard to achieve that moment. That's the best feeling you're ever going to get. They don't come any bigger than that – South Africa, in South Africa, and for the British Lions. Winners.

We went up to the reception in the stadium afterwards and listened to the various dignitaries going over the game. Fran was obviously delighted and was able to thank and congratulate not only us but also the coaches and everyone else involved, including the four home Unions that had made his job as easy as possible and given their support to the selectors and the entire squad. There was nothing the South Africans could say other than that they had been beaten and they had lost the series. I think they were devastated. To lose a home series against the All Blacks is one thing, but to lose another one against the Lions the following year was too much for them to take in at this stage. But we were going to enjoy that evening, as victors should.

The choice was between hanging out in the car park, something so big that it makes the West Car Park at Twickenham look like a patio, or going home. We decided to go home. After a truly great celebration on the coach, we all got together for a drink at the hotel, to savour the moment as a squad before heading out to celebrate some more. There was no better place to do this than Durban, where the majority of our support was to be found. We decided to live for the moment, we would worry about next week on the Monday.

After a few hours in a relatively quiet bar in the company of Jeremy Guscott, Scott Gibbs, John Bentley, Jason Leonard and Stuart Barnes, we decided to go nightclubbing. We met up with the rest of the boys, and most of our supporters, and we all enjoyed one hell of a night. We didn't get back to the hotel until eight in the morning. We woke some considerable time later to the sound of John Bentley screaming out of the window, addressing the whole of Durban with 'British Lions two, South Africa nil'. This reminded me of a fact that I still found hard to believe. But it was true, and it was just phenomenal – out of this world.

South Africa 15 British Lions 18

South Africa	*British Lions*
A Joubert (Natal)	N Jenkins (Pontypridd)
A Snyman (N Transvaal)	J Bentley (Newcastle)
P Montgomery (Western Province)	J Guscott (Bath)
D van Schalkwyck (N Transvaal)	S Gibbs (Swansea)
P Rossouw (Western Province)	A Tait (Newcastle)
H Honiball (Natal)	G Townsend (Northampton)
J van der Westhuizen (N Transvaal)	M Dawson (Northampton)
P du Randt (Orange Free State)	T Smith (Watsonians)
N Drotske (Orange Free State)	K Wood (Harlequins)
A Garvey (Natal)	P Wallace (Saracens)

H Strydom (N Transvaal)
M Andrews (Natal)
R Kruger (N Transvaal)
A Venter (Orange Free State)
G Teichmann (Natal)

M Johnson (Leicester)
J Davidson (London Irish)
L Dallaglio (Wasps)
R Hill (Saracens)
T Rodber (Northampton)

Scorers
South Africa. Tries: van der Westhuizen, Montgomery, Joubert.
British Lions. Penalties: Jenkins (5). Dropped goal: Guscott.

Replacements
South Africa: G Teichmann temporarily replaced by F van Heerden (Western Province; 3–5 minutes). R Kruger replaced by F van Heerden (Western Province; 50). A Garvey replaced by D Theron (Griqualand West; 67).

1 JULY 1997

Northern Free State 44 British Lions 67

The day after our celebration we left to go to a place called Vanderbilt Park, which is about an hour outside Johannesburg. Fran had obviously checked the place out on his earlier visit and it was a lovely place, but it was in the middle of nowhere and there was very little to do there. Now, as much as the management liked to be confident about our chances, and bullish about winning the Test series, I don't think that they ever expected to win the first two. Therefore, they would have anticipated a lot of hard training ahead when we arrived at Vanderbilt Park. It was a bit of a disappointment, to say the least. It wasn't that we wanted to party all week – we actually did want to train hard, to go for the whitewash – but I think we did want to savour the moment a little longer. The hotel didn't offer the standards to which we had become accustomed and it just seemed a bit of a come down.

However, we got on with it. We were thinking of Johannesburg; we were thinking it would be great to go one better than the All Blacks, to beat these guys 3–0, and at Ellis Park where we had already met with success on this tour. So the training went well. It was going to be very difficult for those who played in the second Test to pick themselves up for the third, but it was also going to be very interesting to see how the management were going to respond. We'd won two now, we had one more to go, they had nothing to lose; we, as a team, had nothing to lose.

We wanted to go out on a high, to finish on a really good performance, playing the sort of rugby that we had played in the provincial games. The two Test games had been very close and we wanted to try and play with a little bit more confidence, to be a little more positive when we had the ball. The last midweek game was against Northern Free State, in a place called Welcome. I think the writing was on the wall in that particular game. Our discipline, our professional attitude and our sense of purpose had been our trademark throughout the tour and, although we won the game with sixty-seven points, we conceded forty-four. That showed a sloppiness which had not previously existed. Mission had been accomplished and I think that minds were perhaps starting to think about home now. But, having said that, there was no excuse for such a sloppy performance. We were not a good team on the night and we perhaps had sown the seeds of failure.

Northern Free State 44 British Lions 67

Northern Free State	*British Lions*
M Ehrentraut	T Stimpson (Newcastle)
R Harmse	T Stanger (Hawick)
A van Buuren	N Beal (Northampton)
T de Beer	A Bateman (Richmond)
W Nagel	T Underwood (Newcastle)
E Herbert	M Catt (Bath)
J Jerling	K Bracken (Saracens)
K Applegryn	J Leonard (Harlequins)
O Wagener	M Regan (Bristol)
B Nel	D Young (Cardiff)
K Heydenrich	N Redman (Bath)
S Niewenhuyzen	S Shaw (Wasps)
H Kershaw	R Wainwright (Watsonians)
E Delport	N Back (Leicester)
M Venter	A Diprose (Saracens)

Scorers
Northern Free State. Tries: penalty try, Ehrentraut, Wagener, van Buuren, Herbert. Penalties: Herbert (2). Conversions: Herbert (5).
British Lions. Tries: Underwood (3), Shaw (2), Stimpson (2), Back, Bracken, Regan. Penalty: Stimpson. Conversions: Stimpson (7).

Replacements
Northern Free State. M Ehrentraut replaced by J Burrows (66 minutes), E Delport replaced by A Michau.
British Lions. J Leonard replaced by G Rowntree (Leicester; 40), K Bracken replaced by A Healey (54).

5 JULY 1997

South Africa 35 British Lions 16

South Africa weren't even contemplating 3–0. Losing another home series was bad enough, but if they were whitewashed then I think the majority of their team would have faced execution. They were determined to put the record straight; it was important that they won. From our point of view, the Lions management recognised this new sloppiness and decided to make changes in an attempt to inject new life, new vigour, into what was perhaps now a tired team. Some changes were forced upon us. For instance, Tim Rodber caught a severe bout of flu which obviously ruled him out of the game. Anyway, those players joining us for the first time all got what they deserved – a Test appearance. I was moved to No. 8 and Rob Wainwright came in on the blind side, Neil Back played open side and Mark Regan, getting a close call ahead of Barry Williams, came in for Keith Wood.

When we finally kicked off at Ellis Park, we were determined we weren't going out there just to make up the numbers. We were determined to win the game but perhaps we got over-confident; we tried to play them too deep and we were running it from everywhere, making mistakes which cost us dearly. The discipline which had served us so well in the first two Tests let us down in the third. We gave away penalties and Jannie de Beer kicked immaculately. Before we knew it we were 13–0 down, and that was going to be very difficult to recover. We did get ourselves back into the game at 13–9, but then South Africa responded well yet again. I enjoyed myself because I was back in at No. 8 for the first time in ages. To go in at that level was a real challenge, and one that I relished. We put a lot more width on the ball than we had done in the previous matches, certainly the previous Test matches, and we played some of our best rugby. But we didn't play well enough to win. Late on we were still well in touch, we were only a try down. Then, in the last fifteen minutes, it showed that it was the end of the tour, that perhaps the elation of winning the Test series had spilled over a bit more than it should have done. We were just absolutely shattered and South Africa finished the better team. They pulled away from us and gave the scoreline a flattering appearance.

We were very disappointed to have lost the game but we'd won the series, so it was one of those matches where you don't quite know what to feel. They presented Martin Johnson with the trophy for winning the series, so I suppose the series is three matches and we were the better team over the three games. We duly did our lap of honour with the trophy and went over to all the supporters who'd made it to Johannesburg. Despite the disappointment of losing the last game, no one could take away from us the fact that we'd won the Test series. We were delighted with the way things had gone; played thirteen, won eleven and lost two but, more importantly, we had won the ones that mattered. It was a very special occasion and one which I'll treasure for a very long time.

South Africa 35 British Lions 16

South Africa	*British Lions*
R Bennett (Border)	N Jenkins (Pontypridd)
A Snyman (N Transvaal)	J Bentley (Newcastle)
P Montgomery (Western Province)	J Guscott (Bath)

D van Schalkwyk (N Transvaal)	S Gibbs (Swansea)
P Rossouw (Western Province)	T Underwood (Newcastle)
J de Beer (Orange Free State)	M Catt (Bath)
J van der Westhuizen (N Transvaal)	M Dawson (Northampton)
P du Randt (Orange Free State)	T Smith (Watsonians)
J Dalton (Gauteng)	M Regan (Bristol)
D Theron (Griqualand West)	P Wallace (Saracens)
H Strydom (Gauteng)	M Johnson (Leicester)
K Otto (N Transvaal)	J Davidson (London Irish)
J Erasmus (Orange Free State)	R Wainwright (Watsonians)
A Venter (Orange Free State)	N Back (Leicester)
G Teichmann (Natal)	L Dallaglio (Wasps)

Scorers
South Africa. Tries: Montgomery, van der Westhuizen, Snyman, Rossouw. Penalties: de Beer (3). Conversions: de Beer (2), Honiball. British Lions. Try: Dawson. Penalties: Jenkins (3). Conversion: Jenkins.

Replacements
South Africa: P Montgomery replaced by H Honiball (Natal; 53 minutes), P du Randt replaced by A Garvey (Natal; 63), J Dalton replaced by N Drotske (Orange Free State; 69), J de Beer replaced by J Swart (Western Province; 71), G Teichmann replaced by F van Heerden (Western Province; 73), J van der Westhuizen replaced by W Swanspoel (Orange Free State; 81).
British Lions: T Underwood replaced by T Stimpson (Newcastle; 28), J Guscott replaced by A Bateman (Richmond; 40), M Dawson replaced by A Healey (Leicester; 82).

The following morning, on the Sunday, we attended a party given on behalf of the Lions players, the management, the press corps and everyone that had been involved in the tour from the British side of things. Scottish Provident, the organisers, didn't expect all the players to turn up but, one by one, they slowly pulled themselves out of bed and turned up at this bar called The Outback, and we really celebrated. It was a collective release of pressure – the management, the press, the squad ... we all had a great time. It started off with a lunch about midday and went on until about 11 o'clock that night. This was serious partying. Every single member of the party turned up for what was the culmination of a quite magnificent eight weeks. It was just great to witness the harmony – English, Scottish, Welsh and Irish guys training, playing, singing, dancing and enjoying themselves together.

Having said that, I think everyone was relieved to be going home. The Lions were now history. We had come together for a period of only nine weeks and we had played our thirteen games, so we were now disbanding and going back to our normal lives. However, after a tour like that, we all agreed that adjusting to any degree of normality would take a bit of time – it certainly wouldn't be achieved overnight.

To have been around so many talented players, to have been part of that magical tour, was a great privilege and a great pleasure. One of the best things to come out of it all was the special and lasting bond that had been forged between each and every member of the squad. I'm sure that, in years to come, when I meet another squad member we'll only have to look each other in the eye in order to detect that special feeling that, together, we have been part of something unique and very special. To have come out from the shadow of the great Willie John McBride and the 1974 team and to have overcome the most difficult odds to beat the world champions was fantastic. It was a testament to the huge effort made by every single person involved and also to the ethos that makes the Lions so special. I am proud to have played my part.